EXCITING OBJECT LESSONS
and
IDEAS FOR CHILDREN'S SERMONS

EXCITING OBJECT LESSONS
and
IDEAS FOR CHILDREN'S SERMONS

Jessie Sullivan

BAKER BOOK HOUSE
Grand Rapids, Michigan

PHOTOLITHOPRINTED BY CUSHING - MALLOY, INC.
ANN ARBOR, MICHIGAN, UNITED STATES OF AMERICA
1976

Contents

Call to Worship

We are here at Children's Church
To learn and sing and pray,
To listen as we hear God's Word
So Him we can obey.

Introduction

Children's Church can become a reality if young parents and leaders of the church see the need for such a program.

Mr. and Mrs. Miller are concerned about Kathy, their seven-year-old daughter.

"Is she old enough to accept Christ as her Saviour?" they wonder. "How can we know if and when she has had an experience with the Lord?" Being wise parents, they will not want to rush their young daughter into a decision that isn't genuinely hers. Being concerned parents, they will want to help her to make that decision when she is ready.

Carl, their five-year-old son, is another problem. He is a wiggler. It is obvious he doesn't get anything out of the adult worship services. And, to tell the truth, his mother and father do not get much either! Which is better? To go to church, hand Carl a piece of paper and a pencil and let him draw and wiggle through the worship services (and train him to do the same when he becomes older), or to stay home?

Mr. and Mrs. Wagner would like to sing in the choir. They have two youngsters, Phil, aged four, and Melinda, aged five. The choir is minus two would-be vocalists!

Mark doesn't bother his parents, Mr. and Mrs. Hall, when he goes to church with them. He is well behaved enough. But actually, it is a waste of Mark's time. He isn't learning anything — except, perhaps, to dislike this sanctuary where he is brought each Sunday morning after Sunday School and forced to sit still for what seems to him to be hours!

These parents can become aware that their problems are more or less universal.

They can do something about it.

We solved these problems by initiating Children's Church.

1

What Is Children's Church?

Children's Church is a worship experience for boys and girls.

Many people have many ideas as to what Children's Church is. Some churches consider maintaining a nursery as Children's Church. One minister told me that they had Children's Church; but when I investigated further, I learned that young people were singing in their church choir. To him this was Children's Church! Another preached a sermonette just before the sermon. Many groups have graded programs, or extended services.

Our Children's Church, the one discussed in this book, differs from all of these. After we had worked hard in planning and solving problems involved in our own activity, we felt that we could save other church workers from all the groundwork we had already plowed. We felt that a successful program deserves to be shared.

Our Children's Church is a worship service for boys and girls, ages four through eight. Not long ago someone told me that it was impossible to interest a four-year-old for a solid hour. I'm glad I didn't hear this before we started our program! I might have believed it! Attention span does vary. We know that. So we vary the program, keeping it interesting as well as informative and worshipful.

We feel that anyone nine years of age or older is capable of understanding the adult worship services. We are careful never to refer to our Children's Church as "Junior Church" since youngsters of Junior age are not included. You, however, might want to include them. This could be done easily.

Because we strive to help the children to become accustomed to the regular church services, we cling to the adult order of service as closely as possible.

We sing the doxology, read Scripture (while everyone stands), recite the Lord's Prayer together, take an offering, have congregational singing. We also have an object lesson, an application story, and a Bible story. The entire service carries one theme.

Not long ago, one of our little four-year-old girls saw our Children's Church director. She tugged on her mother's dress. "That's *my* preacher!" she proclaimed.

A sense of possession is vital to the security of a child. Having his own preacher and his own church enables him to meet God on his own level in his own world.

2

What Is Worship?

A worship experience for a child is the same as it is for an adult.

Isaiah 6:1-8

1. In the year that King Uzziah died, I saw also the Lord sitting upon a throne, high and lifted up, and his train filled the temple.

2. Above it stood the seraphim: each one had six wings; with two he covered his face, and with two he covered his feet, and with two he did fly.

3. And one cried unto another, and said, Holy, holy, holy, is the Lord of hosts; the whole earth is full of his glory.

4. And the posts of the door moved at the voice of him who cried, and the house was filled with smoke.

5. Then said I, Woe is me! For I am undone, because I am a man of unclean lips, and I dwell in the midst of a people of unclean lips; for mine eyes have seen the King, the Lord of hosts.

6. Then flew one of the seraphim unto me, having a live coal in his hand, which he had taken with the tongs from off the altar.

7. And he laid it upon my mouth, and said, Lo, this hath touched thy lips, and thine iniquity is taken away, and thy sin purged.

8. Also I heard the voice of the Lord saying, Whom shall I send, and who will go for us? then said I, Here am I; send me."

Isaiah indicates that we must first recognize what God is. Then we must recognize what we are. When we accept God, He cleanses us. And then we are called to serve.

Subsequently, there are three areas in worship:

1. Our approach to God;
2. God's approach to us;
3. Our response to God in dedication.

Children need to feel God's presence. They are able to recognize God for who and what He is. They are able to recognize their own unworthiness. They are able to respond to God in service. A Children's Church worship service must meet all of these requirements if it is truly a worship service.

It is the purpose of Children's Church to lead each child into a real worship experience. As he learns to worship as a child, he will worship as an adult. Many adults have never learned how to worship God.

In order to help this experience to be attained, each worship service needs to have a specific purpose as its goal. Following a chosen theme, all of the thoughts need to be purposeful. Object lessons, music, stories must all lead to the same objective.

If this is done, and if a proper atmosphere of reverence is observed throughout the service, each child (and adult) will be able to worship on his own level.

3

Consider the Congregation

There's quite an age span between four and eight. However, since each child develops at his own rate of speed, fifty children may represent fifty different stages! But this could also be true if there were fifty children of the same age!

Four-year-olds are tiny and their muscles are not fully developed. Even though we know small chairs are more comfortable for them, we use pews. After all, they are supposed to sit in adult pews when they attend adult church with their parents.

Robert wiggled and squirmed. That is, before he attended Children's Church. His father tells us now that he is much better. He has seen a definite change in his son's church behavior.

Four-year-olds are active and impatient. But expecting the best from a child can work wonders — especially if he has a good example set before him.

Four-year-olds often have difficulty in separating fiction from fact. When we visited in the home of four-year-old Denny, his mother told us that he had brought his "nursery rhymes" home to learn. You guessed it — they were the Bible verses we were learning in Children's Church!

Five-year-olds are usually attending kindergarten. They are becoming more self-reliant. They are not so frightened by the new and unusual. They like to share their experiences. They are beginning to get a better conception of what is right and what is wrong.

Both four- and five-year-olds acquire attitudes rather than facts. This is a very important reason why workers should not visit with each other after they have entered the sanctuary. A prayerful, worshipful attitude is best learned by example.

By the time a child is six years old he usually is learning how to read. His world becomes much larger and he can understand better, even though he still lives in the "here" and "now."

Older Primary children grow into deeper concepts and are often able to comprehend their need for a Saviour. Although we teach our boys and girls about Jesus and how He died for their sins, we do not have an invitation in Children's Church. It is understood that any worker will talk with any child if there is a need. The workers observe to see if anyone is under conviction. We must handle this very carefully, however. Primary children have a great desire to be liked. We must be careful that each child who accepts Christ is doing so because of a compelling personal experience.

All healthy children are active. All definitely have a need for love, security, approval, guidance, independence, and achievement. If Children's Church is conducted properly, this activity can be channeled into a program of worship which will fulfill these needs.

4

Goals Are Set

Before any workers or committee members are selected, a set of the goals should be drawn up. With these goals in mind, workers and committeemen can be contacted.

Our list of objectives for a worshipful experience is something like this:

1. Help each child appreciate the Bible, understand what it is, and why we use it.

2. Help each child enjoy his experiences with God and Jesus, as we tell interesting stories taken from God's Word.

3. Help each child learn how Jesus wants him to live.

4. Help each child to want to please Jesus.

5. Help each child feel that Jesus is his friend.

6. Help each child to know that he has a place in God's plan.

7. Help each child have a foundation upon which a conversion experience can be laid when he is ready.

8. Help each child understand what church membership is.

9. Help each child develop the ability to participate actively and intelligently in worship.

10. Help each child learn to find satisfaction in worship experiences.

11. Help each child to learn how to relate the Bible to his daily experiences.

12. Help each child develop proper attitudes toward God, his family, and the world.

13. Help each child to learn to like church.

14. Help each child to learn the meaning of activities of the church such as baptism, the Lord's supper, etc.

5

A Committee Is Formed

The Children's Church Committee is composed of interested parents. Three couples make up a good committee. These couples do not themselves attend Children's Church. It is their responsibility to help the workers in matters not related to the actual services.

It is helpful when these committee members listen to the remarks made by their own children. By becoming a sounding board, they are able to discern both the good and the bad points of Children's Church from the child's viewpoint. They can also suggest themes which should be presented.

The committee is the liaison between adult church and Children's Church. It also helps select workers for Children's Church.

The committee fosters public relations. One of their main concerns is to promote attendance. This is possible through promotion by means of announcements and articles in the church paper, the daily newspapers, the Sunday School departments, the radio. Posters can be made and placed in the church halls, in the store windows of the neighborhood. The committee can see that announcements are made from the pulpit. They can also attend to any mailings sent to the children or their parents.

One of the regular functions of one of the members of the committee can be to place posters in the vicinity of the church saying "Children's Church Today" on the Sundays when the services are held.

One member of the committee can be assigned to inform the Children's Church workers when adult church is about to be dismissed.

The committee can also sponsor Christian Home Week for the church. They may plan and direct the program. No better service can be given to the children than to help their parents provide a happy, Christian home.

Parents' Nights can also be sponsored. This is an opportunity to reach unsaved and unchurched parents. The easiest way to reach an adult is through his or her child.

These Parents' Nights may be conducted with outside speakers, a panel discussion, a movie, or other such type of program.

As mentioned before, the committee works *outside* the Children's Church. Its function is to help the workers in every way possible, and to promote the welfare of the children.

The committee is selected by the church Nominating Committee who can also name the chairman. It is often advisable to allow the committee to select its own chairman.

Committee meetings should be set up as needed, but they should be held regularly — at least one a month. Special meetings may also be called when additional activities are planned, or if any problems arise.

Some of the matters to appear on the agenda of the committee meeting should be:

—a report from the director of Children's Church — attendance, etc.

—a report on visits and contacts made
—evaluation of the monthly programs
—suggestions to workers, such as themes, etc.
—plans for public relations
—assignments

It is advisable to have the director of Children's Church present at the committee meetings. Other workers may be invited if so desired.

6

Workers Are Challenged

I felt a definite call of the Lord to work in Children's Church. Several mothers approached me and challenged me with a new idea. They were concerned about their children. They felt that a Children's Church would be beneficial.

I was interested. I believed that the children could have a more worshipful experience, too, but had never thought of it in any personal connection.

My husband and I discussed the possibility of a Children's Church and what could be done with it. We had had some experience with children, but not along this line. It became a challenge to us and we began to have ideas on how it could be conducted.

As yet we had not been approached on any official basis. We felt that we should wait and let God show us His will in the matter.

We were approached by the minister of education shortly after that. After more prayer and supplication, we accepted the positions as co-directors and set out on what was an entirely new field for us. But at least the horizon was not mottled with any preconceived ideas!

The specific need of the children was a learning process whereby they might learn good worship habits. We did not feel the need for a *graded* Children's Church. What we wanted was a *miniature* worship service.

Workers, of course, became a primary concern. After much prayer we agreed that the number of workers would be flexible according to the number of children who would attend.

There were, however, specific workers who would be needed regardless of the attendance. These included the director (co-directors in our own case), a pianist, an organist, a song leader, two story tellers, a head usher, and a classification officer.

As directors, we planned and correlated all the activities, notifying the other workers of their duties. We also acted as liaison officers between the Children's Church staff and the Children's Church committee.

The director, who sits on the platform in front of the group just as the pastor does, presides. It is good to have a man in this position. He leads the congregation in prayer, reads the Scripture, recognizes visitors, makes any necessary announcements, and leads in the taking of the offering. He retains his position on the platform throughout the services.

The organist or pianist, or both, plays the organ softly before the services begin. He also accompanies the congregational singing. He plays quietly when the offering is taken.

The song leader plans and directs all the congregational singing. She knows songs appropriate for the group. Atmosphere is created through the music. Also, music can be used for relaxation and exercise. Action songs are good, but the song leader should always close the singing with reverent, worshipful music. Our song leader sits on the platform opposite the director.

The head usher directs the children to their seats and also supervises the collection. Each Sunday he selects four boys to take the offering. He instructs them in their duties and sees that they perform them. He is responsible for having the collection plates available and for returning them to the church office with the money. One boy is selected to accompany the head usher to the church office.

The boys go to the front of the congregation, just as adult ushers do. They stand with bowed heads until the congregation has been led in prayer. After they have taken the collection, they go to the back of the room and proceed to their seats quietly.

The head usher may also serve as classification officer. The following chapter will be devoted to that subject.

In order to lighten the work load of the person telling the stories, two persons can do this. We have both a Bible story and an application story. The same worker tells the Bible stories each Sunday, and another tells the application stories. This also brings variety to the group.

Aside from the workers who have specific duties, more workers will be needed according to the number of children attending. We have set our church up to look something like this:

CHAPEL

(7) 8-year-olds	8-year-olds (12)
(6) 7-year-olds	7-year-olds (11)
(5) 6-year-olds	6-year-olds (10)
(4) 5-year-olds	5-year-olds (9)
(3) 4-year-olds	4-year-olds (8)
(1)	Pulpit	(2)

(*Number in parentheses represents the following*)

(1) — Director
(2) — Song Leader
(3-7) — Adult leaders and workers
(8-12) — Youth

In order to work as a unit, workers should have a regular meeting time, at least once a month. Reports of all workers should be made at this time. New plans and suggestions should be discussed.

Workers are important in Children's Church. They must be Christians of high caliber. They must be people whom the children respect. They must love the Lord and want to help others to love Him. And they must love children.

7

Classification

There is no obvious classification of the members or attendance record of the congregation. However, since there is a close co-ordination between Children's Church and the Sunday School departments, this can be done quietly.

The classification officer should have a card prepared for every boy and girl who is eligible to attend Children's Church. This will include those who are members of Sunday School, Training Union, and any other groups of this age in the church. It also includes prospects of these groups.

A good way to maintain an attendance record can be as follows:

1. Prepare a list in a book or on a set of cards of all those boys and girls who are eligible in each age group. In our church we have separate departments for each year. Therefore, we have a book for the four-year-olds, one for the five-year-olds, etc.

2. Have one worker in each department responsible to keep a record of all those attending by marking the list each Sunday.

3. This list should be available for visitation. It is suggested that a master list be kept by the classification officer. This master list can be maintained by copying the records regularly — each Sunday, or at the workers' meetings.

There are many reasons for visitation of these boys and girls. Absentees should be contacted and informed that they have been missed. This means a lot to a child.

Those who have never attended should be visited and urged to come. Perhaps they do not know what Children's Church is.

Unsaved parents may be encouraged to accept the Lord through this contact with their child.

Parents who do not attend Sunday School or church services

can be urged to attend. They can be helped to realize the importance of their attendance. This will encourage the child.

Children who are regular in attendance feel highly favored by the visit of an adult. This can help them enjoy the worship service more.

A shy child feels more confident after an adult worker has visited in his home.

Children who are discipline problems can be reached more readily when they know that the adults love them and want to help them.

The classification officer should lead an organized visitation program.

A classification card could read as follows:

Father's Name _____ Age _____

Church Member _____

Mother's Name _____ Age _____

Church member _____

Address _____ Phone No. _____

Children:

1. _____ Birth date _____

2. _____ Birth date _____

3. _____ Birth date _____

Remarks: _____

_____

_____

_____

In order that visitors have a calling card to leave on their visits, it is suggested that one be printed which will suit your particular purpose. Ours reads like this:

(Front)

CHILDREN'S CHURCH
Ages 4 through 3rd grade.

Calvary Baptist Church
3921 Baltimore Ave.
Kansas City, Missouri

Every 1st, 4th, 5th Sunday
11:00 - 12 Noon

(Back)

	1969				
January	5	—	—	26	
February	2	—	—	23	
March	2	—	—	23	30
April	6	—	—	27	
May	4	—	—	25	
June	1	—	—	22	29
July	6	—	—	27	
August	3	—	—	24	31
September	7	—	—	28	

8

Physical Facilities Are Important

Proper facilities are important when working with children. There are, of course, ideals which may be sought, but workers can do the best with what they have.

We use the chapel of our church. This is the ideal situation for us. The chapel is a small church with pews, an organ, pulpit stand, large chairs on either side of the pulpit, and a piano.

Other facilities include the offering plates, table for object lessons, and an easel for pictures and flannelgraph board. Of course, as other materials are needed, they should be secured.

The whole object is that the physical aspects of Children's Church resemble as closely as possible those of Adult Church.

In the event your church does not have such a chapel, it would be best to use a room used for adults during other periods, at least a room which is not used for the children for any other purpose. Because they have had no past experiences in the room it is much easier to train the children to have a new approach of reverence and respect.

Incidentally, if an adult class room is used, there should be no distracting elements for the wandering eyes of the congregation. All hymnals should be put away, as well as all other materials such as posters, etc.

Since we have some children who do not read, we do not use the hymnals at all. They are collected and put away before the children arrive.

Facilities are important. But workers with ingenuity and initiative can provide the proper atmosphere regardless of what is available.

9
Order of Worship

Because our adult service retains its same order Sunday after Sunday, we also follow approximately the same procedures each Sunday. This program, while its order is kept intact, must be alive and provocative. Each participating adult should be well prepared for the portion for which he is responsible.

The program should offer variety. It should also offer the boys and girls an opportunity to stretch once in a while. When the adult in charge sees that the children are restless, he may use some kind of finger play or standing exercise which will relieve the congregation of the "fidgets!" However, except in a case of emergency, no child is permitted to leave his seat. If someone must leave the room, he is always accompanied by an adult.

You will want to develop your own order of service. Ours is something like this:

Organ or piano prelude
Doxology
Group Singing
Welcome to Visitors
Announcements
Offering
Scripture (with congregation standing)
Lord's Prayer
Object Lesson
Special Music
Application Story
Group Singing
Memory Work
Bible Story
Closing Prayer.

The director is responsible to see that the order of service is outlined each Sunday. He is also responsible to make all assignments.

10

Some Problems Are Solved

When we first began Children's Church, several problems came up. You might also have to face some of the same situations. This is how we solved them.

First, children leave Sunday School with papers, pocketbooks, pencils, etc. They are inclined to play with these during church, of course. In order to eliminate this, we did two things. First, we arranged it so that the children would return to their Sunday School class rooms upon their dismissal from Children's Church. Superintendents in the departments have the children leave their materials in the departments to be picked up after church.

Second problem, we had no place for wraps. Leaving them in the pews was impossible. The children returning to their Sunday School rooms solved this. They just left their wraps there to be picked up when they went after their other things.

Third, the restroom problem. One adult worker (a worker in the Sunday School department works out well) is assigned to each department. In our Sunday School we have two Beginner Departments and three Primary Departments. Each worker, along with helpers if necessary, goes to the Sunday School department, picks up the children going to Children's Church, and takes them by the restrooms.

Also, since the groups are set up by departments anyway, and since they enjoy sitting by their friends, each age group sits in a designated row. The four-year-olds sit in Row 1, the five-year-olds sit in Row 2, the six-year-olds sit in Row 3, etc. When the group enters the chapel, the adult worker leads his group in and sits on the far side of the row. Following the group, we have teen-agers who sit down last on the row.

We here repeat the chart from page 20.

CHAPEL

(7) 8-year-olds	8-year-olds (12)
(6) 7-year-olds	7-year-olds (11)
(5) 6-year-olds	6-year-olds (10)
(4) 5-year-olds	5-year-olds (9)
(3) 4-year-olds	4-year-olds (8)

(1) | Pulpit | (2)

(Number in parentheses represents the following)
(1) – Director
(2) – Song Leader
(3-7) – Adult leaders and workers
(8-12) – Youth

We felt that this was a good way to have Children's Church really be a children's church. The children are all in the group (though surrounded, as you may see!) and do not have to strain to look over the heads of adults. Also, of course, the larger children sit in rows closest to the back. The speakers can command everyone's complete attention because they, too, can see everyone.

Every congregation is a unit unique unto itself. We hope that you will be able to adapt this book to fit your needs.

May the Lord richly bless you in your service.

Offering Verse

Thank you, God, for all your gifts —
For stars and moon and sun.
We thank you, God, for loving us —
Each and every one.

We come today with our thanksgiving
And with our offerings small,
To show you that we love you, too,
And that includes us all!
In Jesus' Name, Amen.

Program 1

THE BIBLE

Scripture: II Chronicles 34:14-22, 29-33

Object Lesson: VERSIONS OF THE BIBLE

(Object: As many different versions as possible)

The Bible is God's Word. God told certain men what to write so we may know what God wants to say to us.

God used many men. It took a long, long time to write the Bible. It took many men.

But now the Bible is finished and we can read what God has to say to us any time.

The Old Testament was written first. It was written before Jesus was born. It tells all about how God created the world and how men have sinned and how they need a Saviour. It tells us that God had promised to send His Son, Jesus, to come to earth and save us from sin.

The New Testament tells us all about Jesus and His life on earth. It also tells us how we may become Christians and how we should act as Christians. It also tells us that Jesus is going to come again. God has promised that everyone who has accepted Jesus as Saviour will live with Him in heaven.

The Old Testament was first written in Hebrew because it was written by Hebrew men whom God chose.

The New Testament was first written in Greek because Greek was the language being used at that time.

If the Old Testament were still in the Hebrew language, and if the New Testament were still in the Greek language, you and I would not be able to understand it. So God has selected other men who have translated the Old Testament and the New Testament into English.

In fact, the Bible has been rewritten several times. Each time

29

it was rewritten, the men did it because they thought they could make the meaning clearer to us.

(Show the children several versions of the Bible and explain to them what they are called. Choose one verse, such as John 3:16 and read it from each version. Let the boys and girls see if they can understand the verse better when it is read to them from the different versions.)

We know that God has spent much time and trouble to give us the Bible. We know, too, that we have many things to learn from it. We should read our Bibles every day so we can be learning what He wants us to know. If you have them, read from several versions. Then you will understand His message better.

Application Story: A NEW BIBLE

It was Promotion Day in Sunday School. All the boys and girls were going to be moved up into new classrooms with new teachers. Promotion Day was always an exciting day, but this year the boys and girls in Charles' room were especially excited because they were going to receive gifts.

They were going to be presented with new Bibles. Of course, some of the children already had Bibles, but this way everyone would have a Bible like everyone else's. And now they could have sword drills and practice finding verses together. And their Bibles would all be alike.

One by one Mrs. Davis called their names.

"Pamela Sprink — Ann Harris — Carol Jones — Kim Starr — George Jackson — Howard Brown — Tina Lee — Tom Kirkpatrick — Charles Moore."

Each boy and girl rose from his chair and went forward when his name was called. They stayed up in the front of the room until they were all standing in a line. Mrs. Davis handed each of them his new Bible.

"I am very happy to be able to present you with these Bibles," she said. "I know that you will learn to love them as you study and use them daily. It has been a real pleasure to have you in my class. Mrs. Jameson is fortunate to be getting such a nice class of boys and girls."

Charles Moore looked down at his new Bible. He loved new books, especially this one. He resolved that he was going to take extra good care of it.

That week Charles read Bible verses every day. He practiced finding them in his new Bible. He also began to memorize the order of the Books. He started with the New Testament. Matthew, Mark, Luke, John, Acts, Romans, I and II Corinthians — all the way through the twenty-seven books.

He learned John 3:16: "For God so loved the world, that He gave His only Begotten Son that whosoever believeth in Him should not perish but have everlasting life."

The next Sunday Charles was proud of how fast he could find the Sunday School lesson in his Bible. He was pleased that he could find other verses, too.

After the lesson, Mrs. Jameson announced, "We have a few extra minutes. Let's have a sword drill with your new Bibles. I see everyone has brought his."

Mrs. Jameson explained how a sword drill is conducted. "At the word 'attention,'" she said, "you must stand up straight with your Bible in your left hand at your side. Then I will say 'draw swords' and you are to put your Bible in front of you with your left hand on the bottom and your right hand on top of your Bible. I will then give you a reference. But do not start looking for it until I say 'charge.' As soon as you can put your finger on the verse, take one step forward, keeping your finger on the place, and standing until 'time' is called. Let's try it."

Charles liked to do the Sword Drill. It was great fun. He was sorry when the bell rang and the class was dismissed.

The next Sunday Charles was hoping that they would have more time to have a drill. He had again spent the week working on finding verses. He knew that he could make a lot of points.

When he arrived in his Sunday School room, Charles noticed a new boy.

"Hi," he said. "I'm Charles Moore. Are you new here?"

"Yes, this is my first Sunday. I'm Harry Drinkwater. Am I going to be in your class?"

"I hope so," Charles answered.

That day after the lesson, Mrs. Jameson saved time so they

could have a Sword Drill. Everyone except Harry, the new boy, had his Bible.

"That's all right," he said. "I don't mind. Maybe I can borrow my mom's for next Sunday."

On Monday Charles was glad to see that Harry was in his class at school, too. And Harry was even happier! It's always nice to have a friend when you go to a strange place.

After school, Charles and Harry started home, discovering that they went in the same direction.

"I guess I will not be able to use mom's Bible, after all," Harry said. "She must have lost it when we moved."

"Say, that's too bad. You can come over to my house and borrow mine sometime, maybe."

Harry did just that. Several nights that week he went over to Charles' house to work on finding Bible verses in Charles' new Bible.

Friday night, after Harry had gone home, Charles went into the kitchen where his mother was working.

"Mom, Harry doesn't have any Bible at all. Isn't that too bad? And, you know, I have two. My old one and my new Sword Drill Bible. Could I give him one of mine?"

"Why, that would be very considerate, Charles. Which one would you like to give him?" Mother answered.

"Well, I don't want to give my new one away. After all, it's like all the other kids' and I like it lots better than my old one. I'll give him my old one. After all, it'll be better than no Bible at all!"

On Sunday morning Charles took both of his Bibles to Sunday School with him. When he saw Harry, he called, "Hey, Harry, come here!"

When Harry came over and joined him, Charles said, "You know, I have two Bibles and you don't have any at all. I asked my mom and she said that it would be all right to give you one of mine. So, here."

He thrust his hand out — the hand that held the new Sword Drill Bible.

"That's swell of you, Charles, but I don't want your new one. The old one would be just fine."

"No," Charles answered. "I've been thinking about it. And I

want you to have the new one. If Jesus were here, He would give you the new one; and I want to be like Him."

"Thanks. Thanks loads," Harry said.

Charles enjoyed the Sword Drill that day much more than he had enjoyed any of the others. He felt good because he had shared with his friend. He felt good because he thought that he had done what Jesus would want him to do.

"After all," he said to himself, "isn't that what the Bible teaches us — to learn about Jesus and what He wants us to do? It wouldn't do any good to have a Bible if I didn't use it! I'm glad that I gave Harry my new one."

Bible Story: KING JOSIAH AND THE LOST BIBLE

This is a story about a boy who became the king of a country. And even though he was the king, he did not have a Bible.

This boy's name was Josiah. He became the king of the country of Judah when he was just eight years old.

Josiah was a good king. He knew that there was a true God — the God that we know — and he wanted all of his people to know God and to worship Him, too. But he didn't have a Bible to read.

The people in Judah were worshiping all kinds of gods, which are called idols. They had carved animals out of wood and had melted gold and other expensive metals and poured it into molds and they had made little statues which they worshiped.

Josiah knew that these gods could not do anything for his people. He knew that as long as they were worshiping these wooden and golden idols they would not pay any attention to the true God.

So, when Josiah was twenty years old, he called his servants together.

"Go out into the land and destroy every idol that you see," said Josiah. "I want all the wooden ones pounded until they are dust. I want all the metal ones heated again until they melt down and are no longer figures or statues of any kind."

Josiah's servants went out. They took big hammers and hatchets with them. They seized every idol that they saw. They pounded the wooden ones into dust. They melted the metal ones so you could not tell that they had ever been little statues.

All the buildings that the people had built to worship their false gods were torn down, too. All the altars that had been built for them were burned and broken into pieces.

Finally, the servants came back to the palace.

"King Josiah," they said, "we have destroyed every idol. We have beaten them into dust and melted them down. We have torn down everything that the people used to worship the idols."

"Good!" said King Josiah. "Now I have something else for you to do. I want the house of the true God to be cleaned and fixed up so I and my people can go there to worship."

The men all worked hard. They dusted and swept and scrubbed. They repaired what was broken. They even put down a new floor.

Then, one day, Hilkiah, the priest, found something that was all covered with dust.

It looked very important. So he handled it very carefully. He blew some dust off. Then he took a clean cloth and wiped it.

Why, it was a book!

No, it wasn't like the books that we have today. They did not have printers then, or book binders, or even paper.

It was a scroll.

A scroll is a long, long piece of paper, or some material like paper, with a handle on each of the long ends. The material on which the message is written is wrapped around the handles. As you continue to write, you unwind the paper. Then you wind it all up. When you want to read what is written on the scroll, you unwind the material.

Hilkiah knew that the scroll was something that the king should know about. He called to Shaphan, who was a scribe.

"Shaphan, look what I have found! It is a book of the law of the Lord given by Moses," Hilkiah said.

Shaphan took the scroll. Yes, indeed, it was the book of law. It must have been lost in all the rubbish. It was very valuable, because no one else had a copy of the law of God.

"I will take it to the king," Shaphan said.

Shaphan ran to tell Josiah,

"King Josiah, there has been a wonderful discovery today. Hilkiah found a copy of the law of the Lord while he was cleaning the temple today."

Josiah was very pleased.

"Read it to me, Shapan," he said.

Shaphan read the whole book to Josiah.

When he was finished, King Josiah was very unhappy. He was so unhappy that he cried out loud and tore his clothes. Now this does not mean that he ripped his clothes off. It was a custom when someone was very sad to tear each side of his garment up a few inches. This meant that the person who did it was very unhappy about something.

Josiah was unhappy because they had not heard God's Word before. He was sorry that his people had not had it so they could have known the things that God had wanted them to do.

"God will be very angry with us," Josiah cried. "We must tell Him that we are sorry and change our ways. Call all the people together. We must read the scroll to everybody."

Everyone in the city of Jerusalem came: boys and girls, men and women. And people came from all over the country.

They stood together very quietly in front of the temple while Josiah read God's Word to them.

This was the first time that they had had the Bible read to them. They all listened very closely.

When Josiah was through reading the scroll, he and the people said, "We will do what God wants us to do. We will obey Him."

They were all happy that the Bible had been found.

Program 2

THE BIBLE

Scripture: Jeremiah 36

Object Lesson: JESUS' BIBLE

(Object: a scroll)

Jesus didn't have any books when He lived on earth.

Printing presses had not yet been invented. Everything that was written had to be done by hand. Because it takes so long to copy something by hand, everything that was copied was very valuable.

The people who wrote, or copied what others wrote, were called scribes. These scribes did not write on anything that even looks like a book. They wrote on long strips of papyrus which is from the bark of trees.

There were no book binders yet, either, so the scribes attached long round peg-like handles on each end of the long strip of papyrus.

When somebody wanted to read part of the scroll, they wound the papyrus up on one end and unrolled it on the other end until he found what he wanted to read.

(*Demonstrate*)

All the Old Testament was written on scrolls when Jesus was a boy. He went to a school for Jewish boys. His teachers read to Him and the other boys from the scrolls. They memorized what was written on the scrolls.

Not many people had scrolls:

First, because they were not many available.

Second, because they were so expensive.

Application Story: JERRY'S WELCOME-TO-OUR-NEIGH-
BORHOOD BASKET

The steady rhythm of the ball bouncing against the wire backstop penetrated the silence of the falling dusk. All the other
boys had gone home, but Jerry lived close to the park. He didn't
have to go in until his mother called him to dinner.

Whop, pang, whop, pang. It was fun to listen as the ball hit
first his hand and then the backstop.

Suddenly, sensing that he was not alone, Jerry turned to find
a little girl seriously studying him.

"Hi!" Jerry said. "Who are you?"

Jerry thought he knew most of the kids in the neighborhood,
but this was a new one!

"I'm Kathy Brown," the little girl answered. "And I don't know
where my house is."

Jerry almost laughed. Kathy looked so funny standing there
with her hands on her hips with that questioning look on her
face. But he knew she didn't feel funny.

"Well, maybe I can help you find it," he suggested. "Is it far
from here?"

"I don't think so," Kathy answered.

"What color is it? Do you know the address?"

"I think it's white, but I'm not sure. We only moved in today."

"Do you know anyone who lives near you?"

"Well, two big boys live next door."

"You wouldn't know their names, of course," Jerry pondered.
"Two boys. Let's see. Jake and Hank Peters live down the street.
And then Chris and Kent Johnson live on a little further. Let's
go that way and see if we can find your house. First, I've got to
tell my mother, though, so she won't worry when she calls me
to dinner and I'm not here."

Dashing off, Jerry left Kathy standing alone. Seconds later, he
had her hand and they were walking down the street together.

They passed Jake and Hank's house first. Kathy did not see
her house anywhere near here.

"I remember seeing this place before, though. I remember
because of the swing in the front yard."

"Well, maybe we're on the right trail, then, Kathy. We'll go on down to Chris and Kent's and see if anything looks familiar to you there."

"Mamma! Mamma!"

Kathy broke loose from Jerry's grasp and ran toward a lady approaching them.

"Oh, Kathy, where have you been?" Mrs. Brown scolded. "I've been looking all over for you!"

"I found a park, Mamma. But then I didn't know how to get home and this boy was helping me."

"Well, I'm sure glad to see you, but I don't want you going off like that ever again. You may not always be so lucky to find such a nice young man to help you!"

Mrs. Brown turned to Jerry. "Thank you so very much. Will you come in?" she invited.

"Well, maybe just for a minute," Jerry said as he followed Kathy and her mother up a little sidewalk to a tiny house sitting far off the street.

"This is our new house. It's not very large, but it is nice and clean and close to transportation. You see, Kathy and I live alone. Could I offer you something to eat?" Mrs. Brown asked as she opened the refrigerator door revealing its emptiness. "We don't have much, because I've been sick and out of work, but I surely feel like I owe you something."

"No, thanks, Ma'am. I have to hurry home. Mom said dinner was almost ready when I left a little while ago. Thanks, anyway."

Jerry told Kathy and her mother good-bye and headed back toward home. They sure are nice people, he thought, but it didn't look like they had very much to eat. I sure would like to help them.

The thought crossed Jerry's mind several times that evening. Then he had an idea.

"I know what! I'll fix them a Welcome-to-Our-Neighborhood Basket!"

He ran to his drawer and emptied the contents of his bank onto the bed. Three dollars and seventy-five cents. He had been saving for enough money to buy a basketball, but that could wait.

However, $3.75 would not go very far on a basket of food, he figured. "I know. I'll ask Mom for some cans of stuff."

Racing to the kitchen, he told his mother what he wanted to do.

"That sounds very nice, Jerry. Let's see what we can find in our cupboard. Here is a can of green beans and a can of vegetable soup. How about some peas? And here's a jar of grape preserves. But I'm afraid that's all I can spare right now."

Back in his room, Jerry looked at his small collection. It sure wasn't much. He mulled things over in his mind. From the way Mrs. Brown's refrigerator looked, she needed help right away.

"I know. I'll call my Sunday School teacher!" he exclaimed aloud, forgetting he was alone.

He grabbed the phone book, hunted up Mr. Peterson's number, and dialed.

"Hello, Mr. Peterson? This is Jerry. Say, could our Sunday School class adopt a family? I know it isn't Christmas or Thanksgiving, or anything; but I know some people who really need some food. . . . You think so? Great! I'm glad tomorrow's Sunday. Thanks a lot! 'Bye!"

The next morning at Sunday School Jerry explained to the boys in his class his idea. Would they help him?

"I think it's a great idea," Jim said.

"Me, too," all the other boys chimed in.

"Well, could we do it today?" Jerry wanted to know. "I think they need it right away. Could you all bring what you can over to my house this afternoon about 3 o'clock? We can take it over together. Okay?"

The boys expressed their agreement and Jerry felt great. He was glad he had friends like this, that he could turn to when he needed them. They could do much more working together than he could do all alone.

After class and worship service, Mr. Peterson's class of boys dispersed to go to their individual homes, promising to meet at Jerry's at 3 o'clock.

Sure enough, as the clock on the mantle chimed three times the boys began to arrive, laden with canned goods and some staple items like flour and sugar and shortening. One of them had even brought a pound of bacon his mother had said she could spare.

They filled the bushel basket Jerry had found in his basement. They put the overflow in brown paper bags.

"Let's go!" Jerry called as he opened the front door. "It isn't very far."

Jake and Chris seized the basket handles and lifted. The basket was heavy! Jerry and Jim carried the sacks.

The faces of the boys were aglow with the fun they were having and the satisfaction they felt because they were helping someone in need.

Soon they turned in on the little sidewalk leading to the Browns' tiny house.

"Mommy! Mommy! Look! It's Jerry!" They heard Kathy shout as they walked up to the front door.

Mrs. Brown and Kathy met Jerry and his friends as they climbed up the two short steps. Tears were in Mrs. Brown's eyes when she realized what they were carrying.

"Mrs. Brown, this is my Sunday School class. We brought you a Welcome-to-Our-Neighborhood Basket. We hope you can use the things," Jerry said.

"How nice! And just when we needed them so badly, too!"

Jerry was a little embarrassed by the squeeze Mrs. Brown gave him — but not too embarrassed. For, you see, he felt too good inside to be worrying about that! He was thinking about how glad he was that he had had the idea to help Mrs. Brown and Kathy.

And he was especially glad that he had his friends who could help him. It had been fun working together. In the Bible God said we should love one another and be a good neighbor. It had been a good project for the whole class.

Bible Story: JEREMIAH AND BARUCH HELP WRITE THE BIBLE

Jeremiah was a prophet. A prophet is a person who tells other people God's message.

The things that Jeremiah had to tell the people of Judah were not things that they liked to hear.

"You are not obeying God!" Jeremiah told them. "God wants you to turn away from all the bad things you are doing. He wants you to stop worshiping idols! Return to God," he preached. "He will forgive you if you will only do as He asks.

"You are going to church, but you don't pay attention when you go there. You don't really love God. You are only pretending. He doesn't want you to pretend to love Him. He knows whether or not you really love Him. And He wants you to obey Him!"

Then Jeremiah continued. "You are telling lies. You are stealing. You are cheating and not being fair to poor people.

"Because you are doing all these things and will not tell God that you are sorry, God is going to have to punish you. There will be a great war. The enemy will come in and will take over the land and will destroy everything in it. God's temple will be torn down. After all, you haven't used it when you could!"

Jeremiah was sad. He hated to see how bad all the people were. He knew that God would really do these things, too, if they didn't change their ways.

The people would not listen to Jeremiah. They went on doing all the things that he told them not to do.

They didn't like Jeremiah. We never like people who tell us we are doing things that are not right! But Jeremiah kept right on telling them God's message.

Jeremiah talked to God; God talked to him.

"Oh, Lord," Jeremiah prayed, "it is a terrible thing that all these people will be destroyed."

"Never fear, Jeremiah, a few will be saved," God said. "And you will be among them. But all have sinned, and they have been warned. They must be punished."

"But, God," Jeremiah argued, "I have listened to You. I have done what You have told me to do. Why must I suffer?"

"You will suffer, Jeremiah, but I will be with you. I will not make you suffer more than you will be able to stand."

The priest put Jeremiah in stocks to try to get him to quit preaching to the people. This hurt, too, because when you are put in stocks your head and your hands and your feet are all held tightly in holes cut in a single piece of lumber.

Jeremiah was unhappy because the people were going to be

42

destroyed. He was unhappy because they would not listen to
him. He was unhappy because the people hated him for what
he had been saying to them. He was so unhappy he wished
he'd never been born.

Jeremiah couldn't help it. He just had to keep telling the people God's message. The Bible says "it burned within him."

One day, when Jeremiah was kneeling down and praying to
God, he heard God speak again.

"Jeremiah!" God said. "Take a scroll and write in it all the
things I have told you. Maybe some of the people will listen the
next time they hear it and will turn from their wicked ways."

Jeremiah knew a man whose name was Baruch. Baruch was
a scribe. A scribe is like a secretary. He writes down what someone else dictates to him.

Jeremiah called Baruch. "Baruch," he said, "God has commanded me to put all the things I have been preaching to the
people down on a scroll. We must get to work and do what
God says!"

Baruch got a clean scroll and his pen and some ink and sat
down, ready to write all the things that Jeremiah said to him.

Jeremiah talked and talked.

Baruch wrote and wrote.

After a long time, the scroll was finally finished.

"Baruch," Jeremiah said, "I can't go out and read this to the
people because they will put me in prison if I do. You go and
take the scroll and read it to the people. When they hear this,
perhaps they will be sorry for all the bad things they have done
and will tell God so."

Baruch took the scroll to the gates of the temple. He read it
very loudly so all the people could hear.

The king's scribes heard that Baruch was reading the scroll.
They wanted to hear it, too. They sent Jehudi, one of their
men, to get him.

"Baruch," Jehudi said, "you must come with me. The king's
scribes want to hear what you have been reading."

Baruch followed Jehudi back to the room where the scribes
and some princes were waiting for them.

"Sit down, Baruch," they invited, "and read the scroll to us."

Baruch sat down. The scribes and princes sat down. And Baruch read to them from the scroll.

When he had finished reading, the men all looked at each other. They were afraid. They didn't like what they had heard. And they knew the king would not like it either!

"We must tell King Jehoiakim," they said. "You and Jeremiah must go hide so he will not be able to find you after he has heard this."

So Baruch went back to Jeremiah. The princes and scribes went to the king.

Jehudi said to the king, "King Jehoiakim, Baruch the scribe has written a message which Jeremiah says is from God. You should hear it."

"Read it to me immediately!" the king answered.

When Jehoiakim heard the words written on the scroll, he was very angry. He was so angry that every time Jehudi would finish reading a column or two of the scroll King Jehoiakim would take his penknife and cut it off and throw it into the fire. By the time Jehudi had finished reading the scroll, it was all burned up.

Then King Jehoiakim shouted, "Go get this Jeremiah and this Baruch and bring them to me!"

King Jehoiakim was angry. He wanted to punish Jeremiah and Baruch for writing the scroll.

But God helped Jeremiah and Baruch. They hid in a safe place, and didn't come out of their hiding place until King Jehoiakim stopped looking for them!

When King Jehoiakim destroyed the scroll, he thought that he had destroyed all that had been written on it. But he was wrong.

God talked to Jeremiah again. "Get another clean scroll," He said, "and write in it everything that you wrote on the first one."

Jeremiah gave another clean scroll to Baruch. Then he told Baruch all the words he had said before. In fact, he even told him more. Baruch wrote them all down.

This book that Jeremiah dictated to Baruch is in our Bible today. It is called the Book of Jeremiah and it is in the Old Testament.

God chose other men like Jeremiah, too — men who loved Him and followed Him. He told them things that He wanted them to say, just like He told Jeremiah. All of these books were saved and one day they were all put together into one big book.

That is how God gave us the Bible.

Program 3

PRAYER

Scripture: Daniel 1 and 2

Object Lesson: BOYS AND GIRLS CAN PRAY

(Object: A picture of a child praying)

As soon as we are able to talk we can start talking to God.

God hears boys and girls just as He hears grownups. He loves children. He wants us to talk to Him. He tells us so in the Bible. We call it "praying" when we talk to God.

We can pray wherever we are. We can pray no matter what we are doing.

It is always good to kneel beside our beds at night so we can talk to God just before we go to bed.

Another time that is good to pray is just before meals. It is a good time to thank God for the food that we are going to eat, as well as for all the other good things we have. Some people call this "saying grace." Some say it is asking a "blessing."

We can pray wherever we are, because God can always hear us. We can pray at school, in the backyard, on the front porch, on the playground, on the sidewalk walking home from the store. God always knows where we are and He can always hear us when we talk with Him.

He can hear you when you just think the words, because He knows what we are thinking, too.

Jesus prayed all the time when He was living on earth.

God wants us to pray, too.

Application Story: CARL'S PRAYER

"Humph," Carl Young grunted. "I don't believe in prayer. I believe that we're supposed to work and get things done by

45

ourselves. God doesn't have time to mess with each one of us!"

"I don't know, though," Ernie answered. "I've prayed and I'm sure God has answered my prayers."

Carl and Ernest were walking home from school together. They had been talking about prayer because they were in the same Sunday School class and the teacher had given them a project for the week. Each boy was supposed to bring to class at least one prayer testimony next Sunday.

The boys liked their teacher, Mr. Titus. They honestly wanted to be able to do what he had asked them to do.

But Carl had a real problem. How could he bring any testimony about prayer when he didn't believe in it?

Ernest made a suggestion. "We should at least try to do what Mr. Titus asked us to do. Let's read the Bible verses he asked us to read. How about coming over to my house right now? We can read them together."

"Well, okay. If you want to," Carl said. "We can stop at my house and I'll ask Mom if it's okay."

The boys turned in at the big white house where Carl lived. Ernie's house was down the street a way.

"Hey, Mom," Carl called. "I'm home."

The two boys followed the pleasant aroma coming from the kitchen. They found Carl's mother taking a sheet of chocolate chip cookies from the oven.

"Just in time, boys. Help yourselves, but don't get burned," Mrs. Young invited.

The boys quickly downed the warm treats.

"Mom, may I go over to Ernie's for a while? We want to work on our Sunday School project together."

Receiving permission, Carl and Ernest each picked out a couple more cookies and hurried out the front door. They sprinted toward Ernie's house. At the corner, Carl stopped, but Ernie kept running as he crossed the street. Carl stared in disbelief as he watched the screeching auto swerve to miss his friend. He flinched as he heard the impact of the bumper hitting Ernest.

The car stopped. The young man who had been driving the car dashed up to check Ernie, who was lying in the street.

Carl reached Ernie at the same time. "Ernie," he called, "are you all right?"

Ernie didn't answer. His eyes were closed and his face was pale.

"He's dead," Carl said. "I know it. He's dead."

"I don't think so," the driver answered. "But we'd better get him to a hospital quick. Where could we use a phone?"

"At my house. It's just down the street. I'll go call an ambulance."

Carl raced toward home, not realizing that tears were streaming down his cheeks.

"Mom! Mom!" he screamed. "Ernie's been hit! Call an ambulance!"

Mrs. Young came out of the kitchen, wiping her hands on her apron.

"Carl, calm down. What's wrong?"

"It's Ernie. He's hurt bad. A car hit him."

Mrs. Young reached for the phone and Carl dashed back to be with his chum.

A crowd had gathered and were surrounding the injured boy, but Carl made his way through the sea of curious onlookers. He hardly realized what he was doing as he pushed his way to Ernie's side. Someone had covered the injured boy with a coat, but he lay very still. His eyes were still closed and his face was deathly white. Carl reached over for Ernie's hand and held it in his own. Carl was scared.

Soon the siren of the approaching ambulance scattered the crowd. White uniformed attendants brought a stretcher over to Ernie. Carefully they placed him on it and started toward the waiting ambulance.

"Who is with the boy?" one of the men asked.

"I am," Carl answered.

"Maybe you'd better come along, too."

Carl looked over to where his mother was standing. She nodded her head, and Carl jumped up into the back of the ambulance. He sat on a little seat which the attendant had pulled out for him.

Police cars and people filled the street, but the loud siren cleared a path. They were soon racing toward the hospital.

Carl sat fascinated as he looked at Ernie and then at the cars on the streets where they had pulled over to the curb to make way for the emergency vehicle. He couldn't think. He was still numb with disbelief.

The ambulance pulled into the emergency driveway and stopped. The attendants carried Ernie over to a waiting hospital cart. They left the two boys alone in the quiet hall.

Soon a nurse joined them and began to check Ernie. Carl stepped back out of the way. He felt so helpless. He didn't know what to do. He had never been so scared in his life.

He thought of what he and Ernie had been talking about just before the accident. Prayer. Ernie said he believed in prayer.

"Maybe I can pray for him. He sure can't pray for himself while he's unconscious," Carl said to himself.

He bowed his head and closed his eyes. He prayed the best he knew how.

"Dear God, please help Ernie."

Somehow, it gave him courage and made him feel like he was really doing something for his friend.

The nurse came and rolled Ernie into the emergency room and left Carl standing there, alone. He was still there when Ernie's parents came rushing in.

"What happened? Where is he?" they asked.

Carl pointed to the room where the nurse had taken Ernie. "He's in there," he said. "A car hit him."

The three of them, Mr. and Mrs. Lawrence and Carl, sat on the leather divan in the waiting room. No one spoke. Carl didn't know what his friend's parents were thinking, but he was praying.

"Maybe God will hear me," he thought. "I know He loves Ernie. And I guess He loves me, too. It sure will not hurt to try, anyway."

He tried to remember what the Bible verses were that Mr. Titus had read to them in class last Sunday. He couldn't remember exactly, but he did recall that they said that God wanted us to pray and hears us when we call on Him. Mr. Titus said God wouldn't have said it if He hadn't meant it.

After what seemed a long, long wait, a nurse finally walked over to the three anxious people.

"Is the patient your son?" she asked the Lawrences.

They nodded expectantly.

"I'd like for you to follow me. We need to have some information on him. He's going to be fine. Only a few broken bones. He's conscious now and asking for Carl. Is that you?" she said, looking in Carl's direction. "You may step in to see him just a minute if you wish."

Carl hurried toward the room where they had been working on Ernie. He stopped in the doorway.

Sure enough, there was Ernie, grinning widely at him. "Say, we'll have to read those verses some other time," he said.

"Yeah," Carl agreed. "But I sure have a whopper of a testimony for Sunday School this Sunday. I prayed and prayed for you, Ernie. I prayed you'd be all right. I know God answered my prayer, too, because the nurse says that you will be all right."

Carl smiled at his friend who winked at him as the nurse rolled him from the room.

Bible Story: DANIEL AND THE KING'S DREAM

Daniel had been taken away from his home in Judah by Babylonian soldiers. Daniel did not like being taken away from his home and his mother and father. He was lonely. He prayed to God.

He asked God to be with him and to take care of him.

Daniel was put in a special section of the palace with other young men who had been taken captive. They were treated well. They were all fed and cared for. They even had teachers who came to them every day to teach them many things. But Daniel and the other young men were prisoners. King Nebuchadnezzar would not let any of them go home.

Daniel decided that he would live a life that would show everybody that he belonged to God. He would make the best of what he had.

The Babylonians worshiped false gods. Daniel made up his mind that he would never worship anyone but the God that his mother and father had told him about. He knew that his God was the one true God.

Daniel had three young friends who were also prisoners. Their names were Shadrach, Meshach, and Abednego.

Shadrach, Meshach, and Abednego loved God, too.

Shadrach, Meshach, Abednego, and Daniel learned many things. They were so smart that King Nebuchadnezzar decided that they were ten times smarter than all of his own wise men and magicians!

One night King Nebuchadnezzar had a dream. When he awoke the next morning, he groaned, "Oh-h-h, what a terrible dream I had. I know it was terrible, but now I can't even remember what it was!"

"Call all my wise men and magicians. Bring them to me!" he commanded.

All the wise men and magicians and everyone who claimed he could tell the meaning of dreams came to the king.

"I have dreamed a dream," he told them. "I want you to tell me what it means."

"O, great king, tell us your dream so we can tell you what it means," one of the men said.

"I can't tell you. That's why I called you together. I want you to tell me the dream and then I want you to tell me what it means."

"There isn't a man alive who can do that," the wise men said. "No magician or wise man has ever even been asked to do such a thing. How can we tell you what you have dreamed?"

"I don't care what you've been asked to do before," the king shouted. "I am telling you what I want you to do now. If you can't do as I command, I shall have you all killed. In fact, not only will I have you killed, but I will have all the wise men in the country killed."

Since no one could tell King Nebuchadnezzar what he had dreamed, his order went out to all the country. All the wise men were to be brought to the palace, and they were all to be killed.

Since Daniel, Shadrach, Meshach, and Abednego were considered wise men, they were going to be killed, too.

But Daniel said to Arioch, the captain of the king's guard, "Why has the king sent out this terrible order, Arioch?"

"The king has commanded that he be told the meaning of a dream that he had," Arioch answered. "But the trouble is that he himself can't remember what the dream was. Because no one can tell him what the dream was he has commanded that all the wise men in the country be killed."

When Arioch told Daniel this, Daniel decided to go to King Nebuchadnezzar.

"King Nebuchadnezzar," he said, "please give me a little time before you carry out your order to kill all the wise men. If you give me some time, I will tell you what your dream was."

Daniel went back to his house. He told his friends, Shadrach, Meshach, and Abednego what he had asked the king to do.

"Let's pray that God will help us," Daniel asked his friends.

They bowed their heads and prayed.

"Oh, God, please save us from this death that the king has ordered."

That night, after everyone was asleep, Daniel had a vision. The secret of Nebuchadnezzar's dream was revealed to him.

Daniel prayed again.

"Blessed be the Name of God forever and ever, for wisdom and might are His. He can do all things. He knows all things. Thank You, God, for making known to me the king's dream."

The next morning Daniel went to Arioch, the captain of the king's guard. "Don't kill the wise men," he said. "Take me to the king and I will tell him what his dream was and what it meant."

Arioch took Daniel to the king.

Daniel said, "King Nebuchadnezzar, you know that the secret which you ask cannot be told to you by all the wise men in Babylon. But there is a God in heaven who reveals secrets. He has revealed your secret to me.

"You saw a great image, O King," said Daniel. "This image was bright and beautiful. Its head was of gold; its breast and arms were of silver; its stomach and thighs were of bronze its legs were iron and its feet were part iron and part clay.

"Then you saw a great stone that hit the image's feet of clay and iron. The feet were broken into little pieces.

"The stone hit the iron and the bronze and the silver and even the head of gold and beat them into dust that blew away in the wind. Then the image was all gone."

Daniel continued. "The stone that had hit the image began to grow and grow and grow until it became a great mountain that filled the whole earth."

"That's it! That's it! That's my dream! Now, go ahead and tell me what it all means," King Nebuchadnezzar commanded.

Then Daniel said, "O mighty king, the different parts of the image's body and head — the gold, the silver, the iron and the clay and iron — represent different kingdoms. The head of gold represents Babylon, because it is the greatest kingdom. Your dream shows that in the future all these kingdoms, even yours, shall be destroyed. The mountain is God's kingdom, which is stronger and better than all earthly kingdoms. It shall last forever."

King Nebuchadnezzar didn't like the things that Daniel had told him, but he believed Daniel. Because Daniel had been the only one who could tell him his dream, he felt that Daniel must know the meaning of it, too.

He fell down and worshiped Daniel. He commanded that Daniel be treated as a god.

"Your God is the God of all gods," he said. "He is the Lord of kings and a revealer of secrets."

King Nebuchadnezzar rewarded Daniel for what he had done. He made Daniel a great man. He gave him many gifts. He made him ruler over the whole province of Babylon and chief of the governors over all the wise men. And, best of all, he didn't kill the wise men of his kingdom. Daniel's vision had saved them all!

Daniel didn't forget his friends who had prayed with him. He asked the king to make them governors, too. So they also became governors.

Daniel, Shadrach, Meshach, and Abednego became very rich and great, but they still loved God and prayed to Him. They lived good, clean lives as God wanted them to live.

They knew that they had all these things because God had blessed them and answered their prayers.

Program 4

OBEDIENCE

Scripture: Acts 10, 11

Object Lesson: THE CHAIN OF SIN

(Object: A three-pound size can painted black, black paper chain, and some black links of the chain.

On the inside of the can, fix a cardboard across to cover half of the inside. When each individual sin is mentioned, drop one link of a black paper chain to the bottom of the can. When the chain of sin is mentioned, dump a paper chain with black links out, being careful not to drop any of the individual links which will be caught by the cardboard inside the can.)

Somehow or other, when we do one bad thing we always end up by doing another and perhaps another and another.

A sin is anything that we do that might displease God.

God tells us in the Bible the things that He wants us to do. He also tells us the things that He doesn't want us to do.

One sin leads to another. We have to be very careful or the first thing we know we have done several things that have made God unhappy.

As in the case of Johnny.

Johnny was just leaving his house to play.

"Johnny, remember what I told you about going over to Wilbur's house," Dad said. "Wilbur just isn't the kind of boy with whom I want you to play. I don't want you to go over there."

"O.K., Dad. I won't," Johnny said as he walked down the front porch steps and on out to the sidewalk.

But do you know what Johnny did? As soon as he got out of sight of his own house, he turned toward Wilbur's house.

Johnny had told a lie. (*Drop one link into can.*)

Not only did he lie, he disobeyed his father. (*Drop one link into can.*)

And not only that, he broke one of the ten commandments — the one that says "Honor thy father and thy mother." (*Drop one link into can.*)

Johnny had already sinned three times.

As soon as Johnny got to Wilbur's house, Wilbur suggested that they go over to the park to play. Johnny had been told by his mother not to go to the park without her knowing it. But he didn't take the time to run and ask his mother if he could go. He just went anyway.

Johnny disobeyed his mother. (*Drop one link into can.*)

This made the fourth sin he had committed since he had left home just a short while ago.

While the two boys were at the park, they talked with some older boys who used bad words. Well, Johnny knew that the Bible says that we should not use God's Name irreverently. But Johnny wanted to be like the other boys so he talked as they did, even though he knew it was wrong.

Johnny sinned again. (*Drop one link into can.*)

Wilbur and Johnny decided to leave the park and cut through Mr. Patterson's yard.

"Boy! Look at that apple tree," Wilbur exclaimed. "Those apples sure look good!"

"Well, we can't eat any, though," Johnny said. "You know it would be stealing if we took any."

"Aw, come on! Don't be a sissy!" Wilbur said as he pulled a nice juicy apple off the tree. "They're good!"

Johnny couldn't stand the temptation. He took an apple, too. He picked it up off the ground. But he knew that even this was wrong. He was still taking it without Mr. Patterson's permission.

This was stealing. (*Drop one link into can.*)

The nice red apple didn't taste good to Johnny. In fact, he could hardly swallow it. He wasn't happy at all, and he knew that both his mother and father would be disappointed in him. He knew that God was disappointed in him, too.

"I'm going home," he blurted. And without any explanation at all, Johnny threw the half-eaten apple away and ran as fast as he could toward home.

He was sorry that he had displeased his parents. He was sorry that he had displeased God. Johnny knew that if he had just obeyed his father in the first place he would never had done all those other bad things.

Yes, one sin had led to another.

Each sin just latched on to the one before until all the sins put together were just like one long, black chain. (*Pouring away from the audience, turn the can upside down so the black paper chain will drop out.*)

Application Story: GROWING UP

"Don't talk back to me, Judy," Mr. Johnson declared. "I'm the boss in this house."

Judy's red face betrayed her emotions. She ran into her bedroom, slamming the door behind her. She flung herself across the bed.

"I hate him! I hate him! Don't do this. Don't do that. I'd like to know just what I can do!"

Judy sobbed until no more tears would come.

"Here, Stinky. Here, Stinky," she called. "Come to me, Stinky."

Her little mongrel wagged his stub of a tail in loving adoration. He followed her into the kitchen where she poured out some dog food into his dish.

Gratefully Stinky gobbled up the nuggets. Then he went over to his water dish and lapped up some fresh water she had just put out for him.

Out into the yard they ran.

"Fetch the stick, Stinky!" Judy called as she tossed a stick to a far corner of the yard.

The dog leaped to obey her command, his tail wagging his whole body as he expressed his delight in being with his beloved mistress.

"Let's do some more tricks," Judy said.

"Sit."

Stinky obeyed.

"Roll over."

Stinky rolled over.

"Speak!"

A hoarse yap was her reply.

"I love you so," Judy murmured into the soft fur as she hugged the pup. "I'd love you even if you didn't know any tricks. But it makes me feel so good to have you obey me and do as I ask."

That was what her dad had been talking about to her not so long ago, obedience. Funny thing, Judy thought. Maybe that's what her father had meant.

Just then Stinky spied a cat across the street. He shot away to pursue it like a streak of lightning. Swish!

Almost before Judy realized what was happening, Stinky was gone.

"Stinky!" she screamed. "Stop! Stop!"

But it was too late. The screeching tires burned to a stop. Stinky had been hit.

"Oh, Stinky, Stinky," Judy wailed.

"Judy! Judy, Baby! Wake up!"

The husky voice of Judy's father penetrated her drowsiness.

"Judy, are you all right? You were crying in your sleep."

"Oh, Daddy," Judy sobbed. "I just had the awfulest dream. I dreamed that Stinky got run over because he wouldn't stop when I called him. Oh, it was terrible!"

"There, there," Judy's father said as he patted her on the shoulder. "It was just a dream. Here's Stinky right beside you."

"I know it was just a dream," she answered as she cuddled Stinky in her arms. "But it was so real."

Judy hesitated a minute. Then she said, "Funny thing. You know I love Stinky. And in my dream I wouldn't let him do something he wanted to do. When he went ahead and did it anyway, he got hurt. That's sort of like us, isn't it, Daddy?"

Judy blinked and wiped the tears from her cheeks.

"You don't always let me do what I want to do," she continued, "but it's not just to be mean, is it? It's because you know I might get hurt if I do it. Like me and Stinky. Oh, Daddy, I'll try to behave better. I'll try to act a little more grownup."

Judy's dad gave her a squeeze.

"Well, in that case, young lady," he playfully growled, "it's time for dinner and you mother needs some help in the kitchen."

Judy smiled and went to the bathroom to rinse her face with cool water. Refreshed, she joined her mother in the kitchen and began to set the table.

Growing up is hard, she thought, but it was good to know that she'd passed another milestone. Maybe she would remember to quit acting like a kid next time she wanted her way. Then maybe she wouldn't be treated like one. And maybe if she acted a little more grownup she would be treated that way, too. It sure would be worth a try!

Bible Story: TWO MEN WHO OBEYED GOD

This story is about two men who obeyed God. Their names were Cornelius and Peter.

Cornelius was a soldier in command of one hundred other soldiers. He was called a centurion. Cornelius was an Italian and he lived in the city of Caesarea. He was a good man who prayed to God and gave to the poor. But Cornelius didn't know about Jesus.

Peter was a Jew and an apostle who had lived with Jesus for three years. He had listened to Jesus teach and preach during these three years. He had been with Jesus when soldiers had arrested Him. He had seen Jesus die. But most important of all, he had seen the empty tomb where the dead body of Jesus had been placed. And he had seen Jesus many times after He had risen from the dead.

At this time the Jews thought that they were the only ones who could accept Jesus as their Saviour. They did not believe that anyone who was not a Jew could have eternal life.

But God had another plan. He wanted the Gentiles — that is, everyone who was not a Jew — to have an opportunity to become a Christian, too.

One day, about 3 o'clock in the afternoon, Cornelius was praying to God. While he was praying he had a vision. He saw a man standing before him. He knew this was no ordinary person because he had not walked into the room like an ordinary man. He had just *appeared!* And, besides that, the clothes that he wore were bright and shining.

"Cornelius," the angel said.

Cornelius looked at the angel. He was afraid. He said, "What is it, Lord?"

The angel answered Cornelius. "God has sent me to reward

you for praying to Him and for being a good man. He also knows that you give to the poor.

"God wants you to do something. This is it. He wants you to send some men to the city of Joppa. They are to go to the house of Simon the Tanner and ask for a man named Peter. The house is by the seaside. Tell the men to ask Peter to return with them. Peter will tell you what you should do."

Then the angel disappeared.

Immediately Cornelius obeyed God. He sent for two servants who worked in his house. He also called a soldier who was his close friend and who also loved God.

Cornelius said to the three men, "I have had a vision from God. He sent an angel to me to give me a message. He told me to send for a man named Simon Peter who is staying in Joppa in the home of Simon the Tanner. The house is by the seaside. I want you three to go to Simon Peter and ask him to come back here with you."

The three men headed toward Joppa to seek Simon Peter.

The next day, as they were traveling toward Joppa, Peter had a vision. It was noon, and Peter was hungry. While he was waiting for lunch, he went up on the roof to pray. While he was praying, he saw a strange sight.

Heaven opened up and a large object like a sheet came down to where Peter could see in it. The four corners were drawn up so it could hold all kinds of animals and birds. There were cows and pigs and horses and lions and tigers and chickens and turkeys. There were many kinds of animals and birds in it.

Peter looked into the huge sheet. While he was looking, he heard a voice. "Get up, Peter. Kill and eat."

But Peter said, "Oh, no, Lord, I can't do that. Why, some of these animals and birds are not supposed to be eaten by Jews. You have told us in the Old Testament that some animals are clean and it is all right to eat them. But some are unclean and we are not supposed to eat them. I have never eaten anything yet that you have said was unclean."

The voice spoke again. "What God has cleansed, you are not to say is unclean."

Three times the great sheet came down for Peter to look into it.

Three times the voice told Peter to get up and kill and eat what was in it.

Peter was puzzled. He didn't know what the vision meant. He scratched his head and tried to figure it out.

While puzzled Peter was still up on the rooftop, the three men that Cornelius had sent had found Simon the Tanner's house. They stood at the gate.

"Is this where Simon the Tanner lives?" they called.

While they were standing at the gate, Peter heard the voice again. "Three men are waiting for you," it said. "Get up and go downstairs. You are to go with them."

Peter went down the outside stairs. He went over to the three men.

"I am Simon Peter," he told them. "I understand you are looking for me. What do you want?"

The soldier answered. "Cornelius, who is a good and godly man, was told by God to send for you. Cornelius is supposed to listen to what you have to say."

"Come in and rest a while," Peter said. "I know you must be tired and hungry."

The two servants and the soldier went into the house with Peter. They ate and rested.

The next day Cornelius' three men returned to Caesarea. With them was Peter and some of his friends who lived in Joppa.

Cornelius was waiting for them. He had told all his friends and relatives about his vision. He had invited them to come to his house so they, too, could hear what Peter had to say.

As Peter was coming into the house, Cornelius ran to greet him. He fell down on his knees at Peter's feet to worship him.

But Peter took him by the arm and raised him up.

"Stand up, Cornelius, I am only a man. You shouldn't worship me."

While they were talking, they moved on into a large room in the house. It was full of people. They were all eager to hear what Peter had to say.

"You all know that it is unlawful for me, a Jew, to come in contact with anyone who is not a Jew. But God has shown me something different. He has shown me that in His eyes all men are alike. I should not call any man common or unclean. So I came to you. I came as soon as I was sent for. What do you want?"

Cornelius answered Peter. "Four days ago about this time, I was praying. While I was praying and thinking about God, an angel appeared before me. 'Cornelius,' he said, 'send to Joppa and ask for Simon Peter. He is staying in the house of Simon the Tanner by the seaside. When he comes, he will talk to you.'

"I immediately sent for you. And I appreciate your coming. We are all waiting to hear everything that God wants you to tell us."

Peter looked around the room at all the eager faces. There were men and women. There were boys and girls. They were all anxious to hear Peter.

He started to talk. "I know now that everybody is the same in God's sight," he said. "Anyone who hears God's Word and obeys it can be saved.

"Jesus Christ, God's Son, came to this earth to live. He had great power because God was with Him. In fact, He was God. I knew Him personally. I know what a great man He was. These other men who have come with me can tell you the same thing.

"Jesus was killed. He was hanged on a cross until He died. Then His body was placed in a tomb. But it didn't stay there. Because on the third day Jesus rose from the dead.

"Many people saw Him after His resurrection. I saw Him and these men who came with me saw Him.

"He commanded us to preach to the people and tell them what He had done. He said that whoever believed in Him would have his sins forgiven forever."

While Peter was speaking, something that we would think very strange and unusual began to happen. The Holy Spirit came into Cornelius and his friends. They began to speak in a different language from their own. Peter knew what had happened, because this was the very thing that had happened to him when he had received the Holy Spirit.

Peter said, "I know that God has received you. Now you may be baptized."

Everyone was glad that Peter had told them about Jesus. They were glad they could follow Jesus, too.

Peter and Cornelius both obeyed God. Because they obeyed Him many people learned about Jesus and accepted Him as their Saviour.

I'm glad that Peter and Cornelius obeyed God. Aren't you?

Program 5

OBEDIENCE

Scripture: Jonah
Object Lesson: DOGS CAN GO TO SCHOOL
(Object: Dog collar and leash)

Some of you boys and girls own a dog. Some of you do not. But nearly every boy and girl I know would *like* to own one!

It might not be so much fun to have a dog if you had one who would not obey you.

It would be very exasperating to call your dog and not have him come to you. It might even be dangerous. You might be calling him away from danger, and he wouldn't even pay any attention to you!

Do you know that sometimes dogs go to school? Not a school like yours, of course, but a school for dogs! When dogs go to school, their masters or mistresses have to go with them.

In school the master learns how to give commands, and the dog learns how to respond to them.

In order to teach a dog to walk beside you and not chase ahead or hang back, you are told to put a collar and leash on your dog. (*Show collar and leash*)

Then as you say "heel" to the dog and hold the leash to where you want the dog to walk, he learns what you want him to do. After a while, a good, obedient dog will learn that he is supposed to be in that place beside you when you say "heel."

Then you can take the leash off him, because he has been trained and he will obey you even though he doesn't have the leash on.

However, some dogs are too contrary or are not smart enough to be trained. I know a dog who went to a dog school several years ago. That dog never did learn how to be obedient. He still runs down our street with his mistress running after him, shouting, "Heel, heel!" That dog never did learn how to obey.

Smart boys and girls learn how to be obedient. They learn quickly to obey their parents and their teachers and God. But some boys and girls never become obedient. These boys and girls disappoint their parents and their teachers and God. They are never really happy, because they know that they don't help others to be happy.

Application Story: DISOBEDIENT CHRISSIE

Chrissie was a little girl who didn't always obey her mother. She didn't know why. She always intended to do what her mother told her. But somehow she didn't always do it.

Mother and Chrissie had a long talk one day.

"Good boys and girls do what their mothers tell them," Chrissie's mother told her. "If you don't, it is breaking rules. And when you break rules you get in trouble.

"Laws are rules. If grownups went about breaking the laws all the time, the world would be a terrible place in which to live. You wouldn't be able to cross the street because the drivers of the cars would be breaking the speed laws and because they wouldn't stop at the stop signs.

"We wouldn't have enough food to eat because the prices would be so high.

"Oh, things would be in a terrible mess."

Chrissie nodded her head.

"I understand, Mother," she said.

However, Chrissie evidently didn't understand, because she still disobeyed her mother sometimes.

One afternoon after school, Chrissie didn't come directly home.

Mother was very worried. She looked and looked. She called and called. She telephoned everyone she could think of and still no Chrissie!

About 5 o'clock, two whole hours after school was out, Chrissie came sauntering in, just as if all little girls came home at 5 o'clock.

"Where have you been?" Mother scolded. "Go to your room at once. You know you're supposed to come straight home from school. I'll have to give you a spanking to help you remember to do as you are told."

Chrissie trudged up the stairs. Mother followed her. Into Chrissie's room they both went. Swat! Swat! Swat! Mother's switch stung Chrissie's legs. Chrissie cried.

"I'll not do it any more," she wailed.

Chrissie tried very hard to do as she was told after that. She realized rules were made for her benefit as well as for others.

Several weeks later, though, Chrissie was walking toward home with Marie.

"Come over to my house to play a little while," Marie invited. "I have a new dress-up doll. You'll like her."

Chrissie wanted to see Marie's new doll. She thought to herself, I'll not stay. I'll just stop by.

But when Chrissie got to Marie's house she started playing with the new doll and completely forgot about going home. At 4:30, she suddenly realized what she had done.

"Oh! I forgot! I've got to hurry home. Mother doesn't know where I am."

Chrissie ran as hard as she could. When she got to her house, Mother was waiting out on the porch. She wasn't as worried this time, but she took Chrissie by the hand without saying a word and marched her upstairs.

"Ow! Ow!" Chrissie cried each time the switch stung her legs. "I'm sorry. I'm sorry. I'll not do it again."

And Chrissie didn't — for a week.

Then, one nice day, Lydia asked her to play on the playground with her after school.

I can't, Lydia," Chrissie said. "My mother says I must always come home right after school."

Lydia looked sad. "I don't like to play on the poles alone. Please come."

"Well, just for a minute," Chrissie relented.

It was so much fun on the poles and the weather was so nice, Chrissie again forgot about her promise to her mother.

After a while, she remembered.

"Oh. I've got to hurry, Marie. I'll see you in school tomorrow," she said as she ran toward home.

This time Mother was in the kitchen cooking supper. She silently turned off the fire and took Chrissie's hand. Once again they went to Chrissie's room together. Once again the switch stung Chrissie's legs.

And, once again Chrissie cried, "I'm sorry, Mother. Really. I forgot. I'll not do it again."

Chrissie really intended to obey her mother. She didn't like having her angry with her. She didn't like having her legs switched.

About a week later, Chrissie decided to walk home from school a different way. She walked with her friend, Doris, for a while, until Doris stopped at her house.

"Come in and play with me, Chrissie?" Doris invited.

"No, thank you," Chrissie answered. "I must go straight home because Mother doesn't want me to play along the way."

Chrissie left Doris and continued toward home.

She saw some girls playing hopscotch on the sidewalk. Now, hopscotch happened to be Chrissie's favorite game. She stopped to watch a minute. The first thing she knew she was tossing the rock and trying to miss the lines as she hopped along on one foot. It was dark before she knew it.

"Oh, my," Chrissie said to the girls, "thank you for letting me play with you, but I have to hurry home. Good-bye!"

Off Chrissie ran. But to her despair, she realized she was lost. She was sure she knew how to go home this way. Had she taken a wrong turn? She didn't know. But she knew that she didn't know where she was!

It got later and later. Chrissie was frightened. She walked. She took turns at corners, and she went straight ahead. But she couldn't find anything that looked familiar to her.

Darker and darker it grew. Further and further Chrissie walked. She was very tired. And she was hungry, too. What will mother say, she thought. But, of course, I shouldn't worry, she said to herself. Mother will be out looking for me. It worries her when I don't come straight home. She'll find me. I know she will.

On and on she walked.

It was very dark now — and very late. Chrissie was crying.

At long last, she saw a building that looked familiar. It was the school! She had wandered back to where she had started! Now she knew where she was. Now she knew which way to go. She began to run. This time she would go home the regular way.

It wasn't long until Chrissie saw the very welcome sight of her home. The light coming through the windows looked cheery and gay. She ran up on the porch. She rang the bell.

When mother opened the door, Chrissie began to cry again. She cried and cried. Tears ran down her cheeks. She cried some more.

Finally, she said, "Why are you home, Mother? Why aren't you out looking for me? I was lost!"

"Why, Chrissie, why should I go out to look for you? I thought you had just disobeyed me again and were playing at some little girl's house."

Chrissie stopped to think. Yes, it was true. Why should Mother have worried? This surely wasn't the first time she had been late.

Chrissie learned a real lesson this time — a lesson she wasn't apt to forget. She finally realized what she had been doing. She had been lying to her mother. She hadn't been keeping her promises. No wonder Mother hadn't been worried. I'm sure I am not going to lie any more, she thought.

And she *really did mean it this time!*

Bible Story: JONAH AND THE BIG FISH

Jonah was fast asleep.

He was tired because he had been trying to run away from God. God had told him to go and preach to the people of Ninevah. But Jonah didn't want to.

And now he was sailing away in a ship.

"Unngh — shoo. Unngh — shoo," he snored.

The wind began to blow. Harder and harder it pushed. Waves swirled upward and then crashed down on the deck of the ship. Sheets of rain poured out of the sky.

Still Jonah slept. "Unngh — shoo. Unngh — shoo."

Frantic sailors tugged and scooted everything they could move over to the side of the boat and pushed it all over the side and into the water.

They twisted and tugged at their oars to keep from turning over.

They prayed to their gods to stop the terrible storm.

But nothing helped.

"Jonah! Jonah! Wake up!" cried the captain. "We are going to sink! Get up and pray to your God to save the ship!"

Jonah had told the sailors that he was running away from his God. Now they asked, "Why is your God punishing all of us because *you* are disobeying Him?"

Jonah shook his head. He shrugged his shoulders. He didn't know. But he did see that the ship would be destroyed if something wasn't done.

"Throw me into the sea," he told the men. "Then the storm will stop."

The sailors didn't want to throw Jonah into the sea. They didn't want to hurt him. They only wanted to get to the shore and to save themselves. So they rowed and rowed. But the harder they rowed, the harder the wind blew.

Finally, they decided that the only thing they could do was to throw Jonah overboard. So they picked him up and tossed him into the dark raging waters below.

The wind quieted. The waves calmed. The rain stopped. The sailors and the boat were safe.

But the cold, cold water closed over Jonah, and he sank deeper and deeper. Weeds wrapped around his body and his head. He held his breath until he thought his lungs would burst.

Suddenly, there was a great SWOOSH and Jonah felt himself being sucked up and swallowed by a great fish!

"Help!" he shouted.

But there was no one to hear him. His voice echoed back to him. It sounded hollow, like he was yelling into a rain barrel.

He looked around, but he couldn't see anything. It was too dark. It was hot, too, and there wasn't much air to breath. He reached out and felt something warm.

Jonah couldn't believe it! He was in the stomach of a giant fish! What a problem! The boat had been saved all right, but he was in a terrible predicament! How was he going to get out?

He sat down to think. He remembered how he had disobeyed God, and he knew that he was being punished for being dis-

obedient. But maybe God would help him, if he asked Him to.
Jonah bowed his head and prayed.

"God, I'm sorry I didn't do what you told me to do. If you will only get me out of this terrible place, I promise you that I will go to Ninevah and preach, just as you said. I'm sorry that I disobeyed you."

For three days and three nights Jonah stayed inside that big fish. Then, slowly, very slowly, the giant stomach muscles began to contract. Faster and faster the muscles moved, until . . . WHAP! . . . with a mighty push, out flew Jonah! Right onto dry land!

He lay there, gasping and blinking in the bright sunshine. What an experience! He could hardly believe that he was safe at last.

While he was lying there, thinking about all that had happened, he heard God say to him, "Get up, Jonah. Go to Ninevah and preach, as you said you would."

Jonah didn't argue with God this time or try to run away from Him. He jumped up and dusted off his clothes.

"I've learned my lesson," he mumbled to himself. "I'm going to do just what God says."

And with a hop and a skip, off he went, toward Ninevah.

Program 6

FRIENDS

Scripture: 2 Kings 5:1-14

Object Lesson: BANDAGES AND FRIENDS

(Object: First-aid kit and bandages)

I have here a first-aid kit. In it are several items which are very helpful if you should ever get hurt.

It is wise to have a first-aid kit in your home.

It is always wise to take a first-aid kit with you when you go on a trip. This is especially so, if you are going camping or swimming.

Sometimes when we are playing we have accidents. Sometimes we skin our knees or scratch our arms or legs. Sometimes we have even worse hurts.

The first thing we should do when we hurt ourselves is to clean the wound. Then we should put some medicine on it to kill the germs. Then we put a bandage on it.

(*Show bandage*)

When we put a bandage on our sore knee or arm, it wouldn't do any good if we didn't take the paper off the adhesive tape, because then it wouldn't stick. We have to take the paper off and put the adhesive tape on us so it will not fall off.

The bandage is supposed to protect us from hurting ourselves anymore on our sore place. It is supposed to keep it clean, too.

A good bandage with good adhesive tape is like a good friend. They both will stick to you!

Application Story: THREE BOYS AND A DOG

Scott, Stanley, and Chris were brothers. They liked each other and they played together very well. They were happy boys, except for one thing. They didn't have a dog, and they wanted one!

One day, while the boys were walking home from school, Stanley saw a puppy in the street. He ran and picked it up.

"Isn't he cute?" he asked as he squeezed the furry little animal.

"Let me hold him! Let me hold him!" Scott and Chris both begged.

"Be careful. Don't hurt him," Stan warned as he handed the puppy over to Scott. "You hold him for a minute and then let Chris have him."

The puppy seemed to like being held and loved by the three boys.

"Let's take him home with us," Scott suggested.

"Oh, no, we couldn't do that," Stan said. "He must belong to someone around here."

But he doesn't have a collar on," Chris observed.

"But you know he belongs somewhere. And it would be terrible if he were ours and someone took him away. Let's just put him down where we found him. Then maybe someone will come looking for him."

"But what if they don't?" Scott argued. "What if he gets run over?"

"Yeah, what if he gets run over?" Chris repeated.

"Come on, Stan. Let's take him. Maybe Mom and Dad will let us keep him."

Scott carried the precious puppy very carefully. He held him tightly because he didn't want him to get away. But not too tightly, because he didn't want to hurt him, either.

"Mamma! Mamma!" Stan called as they neared their house. "Look what we found!"

"May we keep him?" Chris asked.

Mrs. Weaver came out of the kitchen onto the back porch. She was wiping the cookie dough off her hands.

"He is a cute little fellow," she said. "Where did you get him?"

"We found him out in the street. We don't know where he lives and we were afraid he would get run over if we left him."

"He looks hungry, children. Why don't you get him some milk? We'll ask Daddy about it when he gets home."

Chris poured the milk into a bowl. He placed the bowl on the floor. Hungrily the dog lapped the milk until it was all gone.

"Let's call him Lap. That's a good name for a dog. See how he lapped up the milk?" Scott laughed.

Scott and Stan and Chris played with Lap until Daddy came home. They all ran to greet him and to show him the puppy.

"Well, now, boys, he's a fine dog, all right. But you do know that he has to belong to somebody. What did you do to try to find his owner?"

"Well," Chris said, "we looked around and didn't see anybody. There wasn't anyone to ask."

"I'm surprised at you," Dad said. "When you take this dog into your own home and don't even try to find out who owns him, you are being dishonest. It is the same as stealing him. Some little boy or girl is probably very unhappy tonight because this pup is gone."

"I know I'd sure be unhappy if somebody took my puppy away," Stanley agreed.

"But what shall we do?" Scott wanted to know.

"Well, I suggest that you go back to where you found the dog and start going from door to door. See if you can find somebody who knows where he belongs."

Scott, Stan, and Chris didn't want to be dishonest. They didn't want to make anybody feel bad because they had Lap. They knew that their father was right.

Walking back to where they had first seen the little puppy, they began to knock on the doors of the houses nearby. Stanley stood out on the sidewalk and cuddled Lap while Scott and Chris rang the doorbells.

From house to house they went. Nobody knew who owned the dog.

"Oh, good," Stan said. "We only have one more house. If they don't know about Lap, we'll get to take him back home."

Scott and Chris went up to the porch and rang the doorbell. A lady came to the door.

"We have a little puppy. . . ." Scott didn't get a chance to finish his sentence.

"You've found Blackie! How nice! Won't you come in?" the lady who had answered the ring said.

Stanley came up on the porch and joined the other boys. All three went into the house with the lady.

"Come in here, boys, and I'll show you a very sad young man. He thought he'd never see his puppy again."

Scott and Stan and Chris followed the nice lady into a bedroom where a little boy about Chris' age was sitting in a wheelchair. When he saw the puppy his eyes brightened and he put his arms out. The puppy leaped with joy and licked the boy's face. Scott and Stan and Chris smiled.

They could see how happy the boy was to have his puppy back.

"Oh, thank you," the boy said he he buried his face in Blackie's fur. "I thought that I'd never see him again!"

"This is Larry, children. I am Mrs. Martin. What are your names?"

The three boys introduced themselves. They told Larry how they had found the dog on their way home from school. They told him that they had almost kept Blackie, but that their father had said that that would have been dishonest.

Mrs. Martin knew that the boys hated to part with the puppy. While they were talking with Larry, she had a wonderful idea.

"How would you boys like to have a puppy of your own?" she asked. "We have another puppy left from this litter. We had given him to a friend, but the man has decided that he can't keep him in his apartment. He's going to bring him back tomorrow."

"Oh, do you think we could? May we call Dad up and ask if it would be all right?"

"Yes, of course," Larry's mother answered as she showed Scott where the phone was.

Scott dialed the number. "Hello, Dad? We found where Lap — er, Blackie — lives. He belongs to a boy named Larry. Larry's mother says that there's another puppy that a man's going to bring back tomorrow. She wants to know if it would be all right for us to have him. . . . It would? Oh, boy! Thanks, Dad! . . . Okay. 'Bye."

"He says it will be fine, Mrs. Martin. And he said for us to come home now before it gets too late. We'll come back tomorrow after school and get the puppy. We'll play with Larry a little, too, if he'd like for us to. We're lucky. We not only get a dog, but we get a new friend!"

Bible Story: A LITTLE GIRL WHO WAS A REAL FRIEND

Naaman was an important man in the Syrian army. The army had won many battles under his leadership. He was a good soldier. And, besides being a good soldier, he was also a nice man. He had slaves in his big house, which was the custom. But Naaman was always kind to his slaves, and they loved him.

Poor Naaman was sick. He had leprosy, which is a terrible disease. In Israel, when anyone had leprosy he had to leave all his friends and even his family. But this was not a law in Syria. So Naaman was allowed to live at home.

One day one of the slaves came to Naaman's wife. She was a young Israelite girl who had been captured by the Syrian army and brought to serve Naaman's wife.

The young slave girl said, "Oh, mistress, I am so sorry that my lord Naaman has leprosy. I wish he would go to the prophet who is in Samaria. This prophet could cure my lord Naaman so he would no longer be sick."

Naaman's wife loved him. She wanted him to be well, too. She told her husband what the young slave girl had said about the prophet in Samaria.

A messenger was sent to the king of Syria. "Oh, King, we have heard wonderful news. It is said that there is a prophet in Israel who can cure Naaman of his leprosy."

"What are you waiting for, Naaman?" the king said. "Get ready and leave at once to go to this prophet. I will write a letter to the king of Israel which you may present to him."

Naaman had everything they would need for the trip packed on his mules. He chose the slaves he wanted to go with him.

Naaman climbed into his chariot. They started on their trip.

After traveling many days, Naaman and his small caravan arrived in Israel. He went directly to the palace and asked to see the king.

He said, "The king of Syria sends you this message, Sire."

The king of Israel read the message. He was greatly disturbed. "What does this mean?" he asked. "What is your king trying to do? He wants to pick a fight with Israel. That's what he wants to do. He knows I can't cure anyone of leprosy!"

The prophet Elisha heard about Naaman's visit. Elisha sent a message to the king.

"Why are you so disturbed?" the message read. "Send Naaman to me, and he shall be healed."

When Naaman heard about the message Elisha had sent to the king, he and all his slaves went to Elisha's house. When they got there, Naaman sent a message in to the prophet Elisha and waited for him to come out of the house. But Elisha didn't come out; he just sent a message back out to Naaman.

"Go and wash in the River Jordan seven times," the message said. "If you do this, your skin will be whole again and your leprosy will be cured."

Naaman stomped his foot. He was angry. "What is this?" he asked. "The least he could do is to come out and talk to me. I expected him to stand before me and call upon his God to heal me. Why, we have rivers in Syria better than the Jordan River. Why shouldn't I go wash in them? Turn around," he commanded his chariot driver, "let's go back."

Naaman's servants loved him. They didn't want him to lose this chance to get well.

"Oh, Master," they said, "it won't hurt you to do what Elisha says. If he told you to do some big thing, you would have done that. Why don't you do this small thing?"

So Naaman and his servants all went down to the Jordan River. The servants watched as Naaman walked into the water.

One — two — three — four — five — six — seven times he dipped himself in the river, just like Elisha had told him.

After the last dip, Naaman looked down at the sores on his arms and hands. Why, there weren't any! They were all gone! Naaman's skin was clean and whole!

"I know now there is no other God than this God of Israel," he said. "From now on He shall be my God, too. Let us hurry back and tell our people the wonderful news. I want to thank the little Israelite maid who sent me to the great prophet Elisha."

Program 7

FRIENDS

Scripture: Nehemiah 1-4

Object Lesson: A CHAIN IS AS STRONG AS ITS WEAKEST LINK

(Object: Paper chain)

Today we are going to use our imaginations.

Imagine that this paper chain is a real chain made out of iron or steel.

Imagine you are in a very tall building and want to get across to another tall building. There is no way out of your building because it is on fire and all the halls are filled with smoke and flames.

Imagine that you look out of the window and see this chain. Remember! It's made out of steel! It is stretched across the space between the two buildings. It is fastened securely on each end.

Imagine you have very strong arms and know that you can hang on to the chain and get over to the other building by putting one hand before the other and walking over there with your hands.

Imagine that you had the nerve to do it!

Great! You would think you were safe from the fire, wouldn't you? But what if that chain had just one weak link in it. Just one. Why, the whole chain would break and you would probably fall to the ground.

None of the links of the chain could do you any good if each one were not doing its part.

It's like that with people, too. If we want to get something done, we must all pitch in and do our very best. If one person

75

slacks off and doesn't do his part, he ruins the efforts of the entire group.

We wouldn't want to be considered a weak link in our chain, would we?

Application Story: MARTHA JO AND THE SILVER STAR

Martha Jo was lonely. In fact, Martha Jo was just about as lonely as she had ever been in her entire life. She and her family had just moved into town.

Martha Jo didn't know any of the boys and girls who lived in her new neighborhood. And it didn't seem as if she'd ever get to know them.

For, you see, Martha Jo couldn't hear. Ever since she had been a little baby she had been what grownups call "deaf."

At home — or, rather, where she and her mother and daddy had lived before — her friends had smiled and nodded and sometimes had written a little note on a piece of paper for her to read. Some of them had even learned some sign language so they could talk with her with their hands. But here, in her new home, nobody knew Martha Jo was deaf. They probably just thought that she didn't want to play with them.

Martha Jo watched the boys and girls in her new neighborhood. The games they played looked like fun! She liked to watch the happy expressions on their faces.

One Saturday morning in December, Martha Jo woke up as usual. She climbed out of bed and padded over to the window in her bare feet. Drawing the drapes aside, she gasped at the beautiful scene in front of her.

Evidently it had snowed all night, because everything was beautifully white and clean. The whole world glistened and sparkled in the bright sunshine.

Martha Jo clapped her hands. She jumped up and down. She loved the snow. She could hardly wait until she had dressed and eaten breakfast so she could go outside.

At last, all bundled up in her boots and snow suit and gloves and scarf, Martha Jo hurried out into the fresh, crisp air.

First, she went to the garage to get her daddy's shovel. She pushed it along the sidewalk from her house to the street. Then she cleared a narrow path along the front walk for everyone who might be passing her house.

But that wasn't really what Martha Jo had on her mind! Oh, no! She was busy planning what she was going to build in the deep snow in her front yard!

Absorbed in her thoughts, Martha Jo got busy on her project. She worked and worked. The morning passed quickly.

Slowly the white snow began to take form under her hands. Very carefully, she was molding a snow manger with a little baby in it!

She worked steadily, unaware that she was being observed. One by one the neighboring boys and girls had gathered to admire her handiwork.

Martha Jo came to a standstill. She could make a snow Mary and a snow Joseph easily enough, but she didn't know how she was going to manage something that was very important to the manger scene. The star. How could she make a star? And how could she put it up over the Baby Jesus like it was supposed to be?

Just then, out of the corner of her eye, Martha Jo saw a movement. She turned around. Why, here were all the children that she had watched playing games. But they weren't playing games now! They were watching her! This was as close as they had ever been to her!

Surprised, Martha Jo smiled. The children smiled back at her. Then, just as though they had suddenly all been wound up like toys in a toy shop, they began to chatter and exclaim.

"How pretty!"

"How can you do it!"

"Show us how to do that."

No one knew that Martha Jo couldn't hear.

She pointed at her ears and shook her head.

She could see that they were puzzled by her actions.

Then, suddenly, Jim Brown realized that she was telling them something.

"Don't you see? She can't hear anything! She's deaf!"

"No wonder she never came over to play with us," Susan said.

Jim smiled and nodded his head. Martha Jo smiled and nodded her head, too.

Then Martha Jo began to think about her snow Baby Jesus. Maybe they could help her. She beckoned to them to look at the manger. Then she pointed up in the air over the baby and made a sign that looked like a star.

"I know what she's telling us. She needs a star!" Harry exclaimed. "She wants us to help her put a star over her Baby Jesus!"

Nodding and smiling, Harry put on his thinking cap.

"I know just the thing. We have a silver star that we use sometimes to decorate. I know Mom will let us use it. See if you guys can find something to put it on, will you?"

Harry dashed toward his house. The others began to look around for something to which they could attach the star.

Martha Jo was happy. She knew that she had been able to make them understand that she couldn't hear. And she knew that it didn't make any difference to them. They wanted to be friends, anyway.

Harry was panting when he came back with his star and a nail and a hammer. Jim found a narrow board which was just perfect. The boys nailed the star on one end of the board and pushed the other end into the snow behind the manger. The star was hanging directly over Baby Jesus' head.

Everyone stepped back to get a better view. Yes, now the manger looked right, Martha Jo thought, and she could see that everyone else was happy, too.

But Martha Jo was happiest of all!

Bible Story: WORKING TOGETHER

Nehemiah was a Jew. He lived in the palace in Shushan where he was cupbearer to King Artaxerxes. The army of Babylon had destroyed Judah and its capital city, Jerusalem. At that time Nehemiah and many other Jews had been taken captive by the Babylonians.

Nehemiah had been fortunate. He had been taken to the palace where he was trained to be one of the king's servants. Being cupbearer for the king was a very important job. It meant that the king trusted his life to Nehemiah because he was trusted to see that the king did not get poisoned. In those days many people tried to kill the king by putting something that would kill him in his wine or water.

Nehemiah watched very closely and would not allow anyone near what the king was going to drink. Sometimes, if there was any question about the water or wine, I think Nehemiah himself must have tested it. If he didn't get sick or die after he drank it, it meant that the wine was all right for the king to drink.

One day one of Nehemiah's Jewish friends, Hanani, came to the palace in Shushan.

Nehemiah asked Hanani, "How are the Jews who escaped and stayed at home in Jerusalem? How does Jerusalem look?"

It had been many years since Nehemiah had been in Jerusalem.

"Oh, Nehemiah," Hanani answered. "It would make you very sad to see Jerusalem as it is now. The people are poor and discouraged. And the wall that surrounded Jerusalem is all broken down. Its gates have all been burned."

When Nehemiah heard this news, he was very unhappy. He sat down and cried.

"Oh, Lord God of Heaven," he prayed, "hear my prayer. I pray for my fellow Israelites. I confess their sins against you. I confess my own sins, too. We have not obeyed your commandments — the ones which you gave to us by Moses.

"You told us that if we disobeyed you, we would be scattered. That is just what happened. But you told us, too, that if we would turn back to you that you would bring us together again.

"Oh, Lord," Nehemiah prayed, "grant us mercy. Be good to us."

Nehemiah prayed and prayed. He was so concerned that he didn't eat anything for several days.

Then, one day, King Artaxerxes noticed Nehemiah when he brought his cup of wine to him.

"Why, Nehemiah," the king said, "are you sick? You look so sad. What is wrong?"

Nehemiah was frightened. After all, King Artaxerxes was a powerful king, and he had control over all the Israelites. Nehemiah didn't know how he would feel about the problem of the Jews.

But Nehemiah was brave. He said, "Oh, king, may you live

forever! Why shouldn't I be sad when the holy city of Jerusalem is lying in waste and its gates are all burned?"

"What do you want to do about it, Nehemiah?" King Artaxerxes asked.

Nehemiah prayed silently, asked God to help him say the right thing.

"If it please the king," he said, "would you please send me back to my country so I may help rebuild it?"

King Artaxerxes said, "How long will you need to be away, Nehemiah? When will you return?"

So King Artaxerxes let Nehemiah return to Jerusalem. Not only did he give him permission to go, but he gave him letters addressed to all the governors between Shushan and Jerusalem so they would allow Nehemiah to pass through their countries. He also gave Nehemiah a letter to Asaph, the keeper of the king's forest, telling him to give Nehemiah timber for the gates and for the wall of Jerusalem.

King Artaxerxes also sent many men along with Nehemiah to help in the rebuilding of Jerusalem.

The men and Nehemiah all left immediately for Jerusalem.

After they had reached Jerusalem and had stayed there three days, Nehemiah and some of his men got up in the middle of the night to inspect the conditions of the city. He rode around and looked at the broken walls and burned gates. Everything was in terrible shape.

The next day, Nehemiah talked to the people.

"Look at our city's gates," he said. "Look at the wall. Come, let us go to work and repair them. Let us make our city one of which we will not be ashamed."

Then he told them how God had seen to it that he could come to help them.

Many just laughed at Nehemiah and his ideas, but many of the people agreed with him and told him that they would help.

Nehemiah got busy and made a plan.

It was his idea that each family would have a certain section of the wall to repair. He appointed each family to its portion.

All the families got busy and started working.

But Nehemiah and the people had a problem. Not everyone wanted the wall rebuilt. Sanballat, a Samaritan and a very important man, didn't want it repaired.

Sanballat talked to the army of Samaria.

"What are these Jews doing?" he said. "Are we going to let them get by with this?"

Nehemiah knew about Sanballat. It just made him pray and work harder than ever. The people worked harder than ever, too. The sections of the wall began to meet as different families completed their sections.

This made Sanballat angry. He and his people decided to go and fight against Nehemiah and prevent the Jews from finishing their work.

Nehemiah heard about his enemy's plans. He set up guards around the walls day and night. He set up family groups along the walls. They had their spears and swords and bows ready in case they needed them.

The Jews prayed that God would be with them.

"Don't be afraid," Nehemiah told the people. "God is with us. God is great and powerful. He will help us. You must fight for your brothers and your sons and your wives and your daughters and your houses!"

Nehemiah then made some new assignments.

He appointed one-half of the people to work and one-half of the people to stand guard with their weapons ready. Then they would alternate. The ones who had worked would guard and the ones who had guarded would work. Everyone kept his weapons handy in case they were needed.

In this way, the building of the wall never stopped.

Nehemiah called the people together.

"The wall is large and we are a long way from one another. When you hear the trumpet blow, come immediately to the place. God will be with us."

The people worked and worked. They guarded and guarded. They didn't do anything else for fifty-two days. Then, at last, the wall was finished.

How happy they all were.

Each family had finished their section and now all the sections fit together.

The people rejoiced. They thanked God for His help.

They had learned that following God's instructions and working together was a good way to get something accomplished.

Program 8

TRUST

Scripture: 2 Kings 11
Object Lesson: WE TRUST MANY PEOPLE
(Object: Pill bottles)

We have here some empty pill bottles.

Somebody must have been sick.

This is probably what he did. First, he went to a doctor. The doctor checked him over to see what was wrong with him. Then the doctor took a little paper pad out of his pocket and wrote some words and numbers on the top page. He tore it off and gave it to his patient.

The sick person took the little piece of paper to the drug store and handed it to the druggist. The druggist read the prescription on the piece of paper. He put some red pills in one of the bottles and he put some blue pills in the other one. He typed instructions on paper and pasted the paper on the bottles. He gave them to the sick person.

At home, the sick person read the instructions. He did what they told him to do.

Now, we can assume that the sick person is no longer sick, because the bottles are empty. He evidently took all the pills.

Have you ever taken medicine when you were sick?

Have you ever thought about the fact that you were trusting someone when you took the medicine that they gave you? First, you had to trust the doctor to find out what was wrong with you. Then, you had to trust the doctor to know what kind of medicine was best for you. Then, you had to trust the druggist to know how to fill the doctor's prescription. And you probably had to trust your mother or daddy to remember to give you the medicine at the right time.

We trust people all the time. If we can trust the doctor and the druggist and many other people, we know that we can trust God, because His Word is always true.

Application Story: BOY ON A LEDGE

Larry and Bob were brothers. They enjoyed going out in the country to visit Aunt Leola and Uncle Hank. They had come for a two-week vacation and this was their first day. After breakfast, they helped Uncle Hank with the chores.

"Thanks, boys," Uncle Hank said. "But that's all for now. Why don't you go exploring out in the woods? Aunt Leola will pack you a lunch and you can have a picnic."

"Thanks, Uncle Hank. That's a great idea," the boys called as they raced toward the house.

Evidently Aunt Leola knew boys pretty well, because she met them at the kitchen door with two brown paper sacks in her hands.

"Hi, boys! Need these?" she asked as she handed each of them a sack.

"You're swell, Aunt Leola," Bob said, kissing her on the cheek.

"This'll taste great out in the woods," Larry added as he planted a kiss on Aunt Leola's other cheek.

Carrying their lunches, they headed toward the woods adjoining Uncle Hank's cornfield.

"Now, be careful you don't get hurt or lost," Aunt Leola called after them.

It was fun poking around among the trees. They looked at the plants and listened to the birds singing above their heads. Very carefully they marked their path as they went along so they could find their way back to the farm.

Every once in a while a rabbit or a chipmunk would scamper by. They joyfully watched for signs of the little animals.

When they reached a clearing, they stopped and rested and looked all around them.

"It sure is swell of Aunt Leola and Uncle Hank to let us come stay with them for a while this summer," Bob said.

"Yeah, we're lucky," Larry agreed.

Deeper and deeper into the woods the boys wandered. They

climbed trees to see how far away they were from Uncle Hank's. They tossed pebbles into the sparkling stream that gurgled in and out among the trees.

Shortly before noon, they decided to eat their lunches.

Aunt Leola had remembered that peanut butter and jelly sandwiches were their favorite. And she had included hard boiled eggs, pickles, and apples. A big piece of chocolate cake was their dessert. She had put a little whistle in each sack, too.

The boys enjoyed blowing on their whistles after they had eaten.

"That was a good picnic. Aunt Leola sure is thoughtful, isn't she?" Bob asked.

"Yeah. Let's go on up that hill there. Okay?"

Slowly the two boys made their way up the hill. At the top it came to a sharp stop. It was a cliff that dropped straight down to a ledge and then on to the stream which had become fairly large at this point.

"Be careful," Larry warned. "A person could get hurt real bad if he fell from here."

Just then, Bob heard a rustling noise. He looked down at his feet to see a big black snake coiled and looking up at him with unblinking eyes. Startled, he stepped back, forgetting where he was.

Larry watched Bob drop out of sight. Frightened, he peered over the edge of the precipice. Bob had fallen to the narrow ledge below and was clinging to a small tree.

"Are you all right?" Larry called.

"Yes, but I sure was lucky. I think maybe I've broken my arm because it sure hurts. How'm I going to get up from here?"

Larry looked around. He couldn't find a thing that would help. "I guess I'll have to go get Uncle Hank. Will you be all right until we get back?"

"Yes, but hurry," Bob yelled up. "It's no fun standing on this narrow ledge with this little tree being the only thing keeping me from falling!"

Quickly, Larry turned toward the farm. He ran as fast as he could. He was glad they had marked the trees. Now he could follow them easily. It wasn't hard at all to find his way.

In and out among the brush he pushed. He knew he was

getting scratches on his face because he could feel them. He could see the ones on his hands.

It seemed much farther going back. He trotted along, carefully following the marked trees, scarcely paying any attention to anything else.

Larry didn't see the hole that tripped him. It wasn't large.

He cried out in pain. When he tried to get up, he moaned. His left ankle was sprained. He needed help. Ooh. Ooh. Now they were in real trouble. How was he going to get help for Bob and himself? "Please, God," he prayed, "help me."

He groaned as he moved about to see if he could find something to use for a crutch. Spying a rather stout stick, he tried it out to see if it could hold his weight. It seemed to be all right.

Progress became slow for Larry now. He couldn't go fast no matter how hard he tried. But it wasn't long until he realized that he wasn't too far from the cornfield. He sure hoped Uncle Hank was nearby. He thought of the whistle Aunt Leola had put in his lunch.

"Whee-ee-ee," he blew. "Whee-ee-ee."

Continuing his slow pace, he kept blowing the whistle.

"Please, God, make Uncle Hank hear me," he prayed.

Crippling along, he finally got to the end of the woods. Sure enough, Uncle Hank was walking toward him. When he didn't see Bob, his walk changed to a trot. The trot became a run when he saw that Larry was injured.

"What's the matter? What happened?" he asked.

"It's Bob. He fell off onto a ledge. He's hanging on to a little tree. He might fall any minute. He needs help."

"I'll go get a rope. Be right back," Uncle Hank said as he headed for the barn. "Leola, Leola," he called.

When Aunt Leola heard him, she came to see what he wanted.

"Come, help Larry. I have to go get Bob," Uncle Hank told her.

As Uncle Hank hurried toward the woods, Larry explained loudly, "Follow the trail we made. We took a chip off trees along our path. See, there's the first one. You can't miss it."

"Okay. I think I know where the ledge is. But I'll follow your trail just to be sure."

Soon Uncle Hank was out of sight and Aunt Leola was helping Larry toward the house.

"It hurts pretty bad. But I had to make it back so Bob could
get help."

"You did a fine job, Larry," Aunt Leola commended. "We'll
have that ankle fixed up in no time."

Meanwhile, Uncle Hank was running toward Bob and the
ledge. It seemed like hours to Bob, but actually it had not been
very long since Larry had left to get help.

"Hi, Boy!" Uncle Hank called down to him when he spied his
nephew. "Hang on just a little longer and we'll have you up
here in no time. You hurt?"

"My arm. But it's not too bad. I'm sure glad to see you!"

Deftly Uncle Hank tied a circle in one end of his thick rope.
He tied the other end around his waist.

"Here's what I want you to do," he told Bob. "I'm dropping
one end of a rope to you. You put it around your waist and I'll
pull you out. Okay?"

He dropped the rope and Bob very carefully obeyed his instructions.

"Now you trust me, boy. I won't drop you. Just hang on."

Uncle Hank drew the rope around a tree to give him more
leverage. Then he began to pull. Heave. Heave. Heave.

Soon Bob's head appeared over the edge, then his body, then
he was in full sight. He pulled up onto the top of the cliff.

"Boy! Am I glad to get off that ledge!" he panted. "Thanks
loads, Uncle Hank! Where's Larry?"

"Well, he had a little accident and hurt his ankle. But he's
okay."

Bob had prayed while he had been waiting on that narrow
ledge with the long drop beneath it. He had put his trust in
God, and God had sent him help.

He had put his trust in his brother Larry, too, to get help.
And he had put his trust in his Uncle Hank not to drop him when
he pulled him up to safety.

Yes, indeed, Bob had much to be thankful for. His trust in
God, his trust in Larry, and his trust in Uncle Hank had all been
rewarded.

Bible Story: JOASH, THE BOY KING

"Wa-a-ah! Wa-a-ah!" Joash cried.

He was only a little baby, but he knew that something was wrong.

"Wa-a-ah! Wa-a-ah!" he cried.

No one paid any attention to him. All the palace servants were running around. They were frightened. They were scurrying from one end of the palace to the other. They were weeping and wringing their hands.

Joash cried louder. He kicked off the pretty silk covers. Why didn't somebody come?

After a while, he heard someone opening the nursery door.

He listened.

People were whispering.

"Sh-h. Be quiet!"

Joash stopped crying.

His auntie picked him up and held him close to her. She wrapped him in a blanket and covered his face.

Where was Auntie Jehosheba taking him? And why was she tiptoeing so quietly? Why had she covered his face? He could hardly breath!

Joash was too little to know it, but Queen Athaliah wanted to kill him. Jehosheba was taking him away so the wicked queen could not find him.

Joash felt safe in Aunt Jehosheba's arms. She was a good aunt. He knew she would take care of him.

After a while, they arrived at the house of Jehosheba and Jehoiada, her husband, the high priest.

"We shall hide him until he is old enough to be crowned king," Jehoida said.

Joash liked living with his aunt and uncle. They were very kind to him.

There weren't any other children, but he enjoyed playing with his nurse.

Jehoiada and Jehosheba taught him to read and to write.

They told him about God.

They told him many stories. He especially liked the one about a little boy whose name was Moses. Moses had been hidden away just like Joash. Then he had been rescued, too. And he had grown up to be a great man who loved and followed God.

"I will grow up and be a good man and follow God, too," Joash said.

One day, when Joash was seven years old, Jehoiada said to him, "Joash, I have something very important to tell you. Today you will be crowned king of Judah."

Joash dressed up in the beautiful clothes Joehoiada gave him. How nice he looked!

He was excited as he looked out into the street. There were many people. They were as far as he could see. Many of them were soldiers.

They were all waiting for Joash.

He felt very important.

Some of the people were guarding the gates and the doors.

Some of them came to take Joash and Jehoiada to the temple. Joash walked as straight and as tall as a seven-year-old boy could as he was led into the inner court of the temple.

The crowd watched quietly as Jehoiada placed the crown on Joash's head. Then the people began to shout and cheer.

Joash felt proud and happy.

"Now you are king," the high priest said. "Be a good king and follow God's laws."

Joash looked at all the people.

He looked at his uncle.

"Oh, Jehoiada, I am only seven years old! I don't know how to be a king!"

"Don't worry," said Jehoiada. "I will help you. And God will help you, too."

Joash reached up to touch the heavy crown that was sitting on his head.

"Thank you, Jehoiada. I will do my best to be a good king."

Program 9

TRUST

Scripture: Acts 6, 7

Object Lesson: CHARGE IT, PLEASE!

(Object: Promissory note, charge-a-plate)

Even grownups do not always have all the money they would like to have! Sometimes they want to buy things and they do not have the money to pay for them.

Mr. Brown might want to buy a car or some furniture. Mr. and Mrs. Jones might want to buy a house.

Most people do not have enough money in the bank to pay for large items like these.

Sometimes grownups can use a charge-a-plate when they want to purchase something at a store. Then they pay for the item when they receive their bill at the end of the month. If a store lets a person have a charge account, this means that the store trusts him. The store owner believes that the buyer will pay when he gets his bill.

When people buy large items like a car or a house, they usually can't pay for all of it at the end of the month, either. There is another way that they can pay for it — on time. This means that they can make payments on it each month.

Most new cars cost more than $2000. Hardly anyone has that much cash! And houses cost even more! So grownups usually buy their cars and houses on time, making monthly payments. They sign a promissory note, stating that they will pay monthly, and how much they will pay. This means that they promise to make their payments.

When people trust you, they believe what you say.

Boys and girls are too young to have charge accounts and to sign promissory notes, but they can be trustworthy. This means that whatever they say is true and honest. It means that they will not take anything that does not belong to them. It means that when they make a promise they will do their very best to keep that promise.

We can always trust God. And God wants us to be trustworthy, too.

Application Story: A SPECIAL SATURDAY

John was excited! This Saturday was going to be a very special Saturday. He and his dad were going to spend it together.

Dad was out of town so much of the time that they didn't get to do this often.

Last time they had gone to a baseball game. John had munched on so many hot dogs and downed so many root beers that he didn't get over that outing for several days!

The time before that, they had gone to the zoo and spent the afternoon ambling from one cage to another. They had stopped for hamburgers and malts on the way home.

They always had lots of fun. Dad was really a swell guy. John didn't know any other kid who had a dad half as good as his.

Today was Friday. All week John had tried to think up a super dooper for Saturday. Then he remembered! The circus was in town! Boy! How lucky!

Walking home from school, absorbed in his own thoughts, John didn't notice the other boys across the street.

"Hey, John!" one of them called. "Come on over!"

John crossed the street and joined the group. Then he realized what was happening. They were picking on Frank Douglas again.

"Look at old sissy Frankie here," teased Harry, the biggest of the boys. "Him's mamma made him wear him's bootsies today."

Frank, who was younger than the others and small for his age at that, wanted to run; but the boys blocked him as he tried to dart out from among them.

"What's the matter, Frankie? Wanno go home to mamma?"

"Aw, leave him alone, Harry," John interrupted. "He hasn't done anything to you."

"We like to see him cry. Don't we, Frankie? Run along, Frankie. Go to mamma."

Frank dashed out of the group as soon as they opened a way. He ran toward his home, trying not to show how upset he was.

"That's not right, Harry," John reprimanded the leader. "You shouldn't tease Frank. He has a hard enough time as it is."

"Aw, lay off, John. We didn't call you over to have you preach to us!"

The boys split up to go their respective ways. John's mind returned to his thoughts about Saturday and the circus as he directed his steps toward home.

When he passed Frank's house, he saw Frank sitting on the front porch steps, his head on his knees.

"Hey, Frank, don't let those guys get your goat," John called. "They just need to pick on somebody."

"I know it," Frank answered. "But I sure hate to have them pick on me. Thanks for taking my side, though, John."

"Aw, it wasn't anything. Your mom home yet?"

"No, but she'll be here pretty quick."

Frank's mother worked. He didn't have a father. John thought it really was a shame. It was nice to have his own mother home when school was out. He knew Frank missed his. And, boy, to have no dad would be terrible. Then John remembered their plans for Saturday.

"Say, Frank, how would you like to go to the circus with my dad and me tomorrow?" He knew Dad would say it was all right.

Frank's eyes caught some of the excitement shining in John's. Then he remembered.

"That would really be swell, John, but I have to take care of Cindy tomorrow because Mom has to work."

Cindy was Frank's little sister. She stayed with the baby sitter during the week, but Frank watched her when his mother had to work on Saturdays.

"That's too bad," John said. "Maybe some other time. Okay?"

It was beginning to get late and John hurried on so he could be home when his dad arrived. He ran to the garage so he could walk into the house with him.

"Hey, Dad, how about our going to the circus tomorrow?" John asked.

"Sounds fine to me, Son," Dad replied.

Then John told him all about Frank.

"It would be nice to take him with us to the circus. It's too bad he has to take care of his little sister," Dad responded. "Why don't you and I walk up to Frank's for a minute? Dinner isn't ready yet. We'll tell your mother we'll be right back."

John and his dad knocked on Frank's front door. John didn't have the least idea what his father had in mind. Frank's mother answered.

"Hello, Mrs. Douglas. I'm John Johnson's father. Could you have a minute for us to talk with you?"

"Why, of course, do come in," Mrs. Douglas invited. "Please sit down, Mr. Johnson. Is something wrong?"

"Why, no, of course not. It's just that John and I plan to go to the circus tomorrow and we were wondering if Frank and Cindy could go with us."

Frank and Cindy both! Boy! That's a great idea, John thought. His dad was really smart.

"Oh, that would be lovely," Mrs. Douglas answered. "Thank you, Mr. Johnson. I know they'd love to go. They miss so many things because I can't take them. They miss having their father, too."

"Well, they won't have to miss the circus, anyway!" John chimed in.

Now they could all go to the circus together. This would really be a special Saturday. John was happy to be able to share his dad. It was fun to have him all to himself, but it would be more fun to be able to share him with Frank and Cindy, who had no father of their own. It might even be fun to pretend he was their big brother, too. They sure needed one!

Bible Story: STEPHEN, A COURAGEOUS DEACON

Stephen was a deacon. He was chosen by the twelve apostles after Jesus died and rose again. These apostles were so busy that they needed help. They didn't have time to take care of all the things that had to be done.

Stephen and six other men were chosen to be their helpers.

After the seven men were chosen, the apostle ordained them. The new deacons knelt down. The apostles placed their hands on the heads of the deacons, one by one. They asked God to bless them.

The story of Jesus continued to spread with the help of these new deacons. More and more people accepted Jesus as their Saviour.

Stephen told many people about Jesus. He performed many wonderful miracles, too.

One day, while he was in a synagogue, he was talking to the people. Some bad men grabbed him and dragged him before the council. The council was the same group of men that had had Jesus crucified.

The bad men lied to the council. They claimed that Stephen was saying evil things against God and against Moses.

There were seventy-one men on this council. They all looked at Stephen. Stephen's face looked like the face of an angel.

The high priest asked him, "Is it true what these men say? Have you been speaking against God and against Moses?"

Stephen answered the high priest. He told him all about Abraham and Isaac and Joseph and Moses and how God had promised the Jews a Saviour. He told them Jesus was that Saviour.

The council refused to believe Stephen.

They became very angry. They gnashed their teeth. But Stephen was not afraid. He knew that God was with him.

He looked up into heaven, and he said, "Look! I see heaven opened! I can see Jesus! He is standing on the right hand of God!"

The council couldn't stand it any longer. They screamed and they yelled. They put their hands over their ears. They didn't want to hear any more. They rushed at Stephen. They grabbed him and dragged him outside the city wall. They threw stones at him — big stones and little stones, big rocks and little rocks. They threw the stones as hard as they could. They threw and threw.

The stones hit Stephen and hurt him.

He knelt down. He prayed to God. "Receive my spirit, Lord. Don't hold this sin against these people."

Then he died, and his soul went to be with Jesus.

Stephen was a brave man. He knew what was right. He loved Jesus. He gave his life because of that love.

Program 10

TRUST

Scripture: Genesis 1; Luke 2

Object Lesson: THE BIBLE IS GOD'S WORD

(Object: Bible)

The Bible is a good example when we want to remember something about "trust." When we trust someone, it means that we believe what they say.

God tells us many things in the Bible. He makes many promises. We know that God has already kept many of those promises. We know that He will keep the rest of them.

God has made a very important promise to us. In John 3:16 God says: "God so loved the world that He gave His only begotten Son that whosoever believeth in Him should not die but have everlasting life."

Here God has promised us everlasting life if we believe in Jesus. We must believe that Jesus is the Son of God, that He was born, that He lived, that He died on the cross, and that He took our sins upon Him. We must believe that Jesus overcame death when He came back to life. It means that if we let Jesus come into our hearts when our bodies die our souls will go to heaven to be with Him.

> God said it!
> Jesus did it!
> I believe it!

Application Story: A SCORPION BITES MALI

Indira's almond-shaped eyes sparkled as she swung her baby brother up to her hip. She loved Mali very much. Perhaps it was because she had helped care for him ever since he had been a tiny baby.

Mali was a good boy and Indira hugged him close to her. She didn't mind having him as her responsibility. In fact, since all girls of India were expected to care for their younger brothers and sisters, she rather took it for granted.

"Oh, Mali," Indira said as she squeezed him, "I will always take good care of you. I promise I will always do my best to see that nothing bad happens to you."

The features of their faces were rounded and soft. Mali and Indira both had dark brown skin and black hair, like most of the people in Southern India.

Indira, dressed in her bright skirt and blouse, sometimes helped her mother spin on the wooden spinning wheel in the courtyard outside their two-room mud house with the thatched roof. She helped cook in the courtyard, too. It was dark and stuffy inside because there were no windows and only one door.

Indira liked best of all to go down to the pond where the big black and brown water buffaloes wallowed in the muddy water. Mali liked to go there, too. He happily paddled around with his friends while his sister did the family laundry.

Today Mali and Indira circled around the missionary hut on their way to the pond. Their father and mother had warned Indira to stay away from the white people who had come to tell them about their God. They spoke of something they called eternal life. This confused her. How could people live forever as themselves, Indira thought. Everyone knew that after you died you came back to earth in another form. This is what her parents had taught her and they should know. That was why all Indians are vegetarians. They surely wouldn't want to be guilty of eating a relative!

The white man and the white lady smiled at Indira and Mali as they passed. The couple was talking very seriously with the holy man whose yellow turban kept shaking and bobbing as he argued with them.

Indira reached the pond. After she had taken Mali to where the other children were splashing around, she joined her own friends. She dipped a cloth into the dirty water. She drew it out and folded it into a narrow strip. Whack! Whack! She brought it down with all her might upon a rock. After a while she laid it out on the parched grass to dry.

"Come, Mali," Indira called when she had finished her work. "We'll come back to get our things later."

Mali paddled up to his sister. Stepping out of the pond, he reached up to Indira. She stooped to pick him up.

"Ow! Ow!" he screamed.

"What's wrong? Oh! It's a scorpion!"

Indira grabbed her little brother up and hurried as fast as she could to the house. She laid him on a pallet on the floor.

"Mother! Father! Come quickly! Mali has been bitten by a scorpion!"

Indira gasped for breath. Mother and father both came running.

They all knew that a scorpion's bite is deadly.

"Quick, call the holy man," Father told Indira.

Soon Indira and the holy man were looking down at Mali who was crying out in fear and pain. He foot was beginning to redden already.

Everyone in the village began to gather around Mali now.

"A slate and paint!" the holy man demanded.

Someone handed him a slate, a jar of white paint, and a brush. Slowly he sketched a picture of a scorpion on the slate. Then he touched the drawing to the bite, chanting all the while. He struck the slate. Bam! Bam!

But Mali's foot was redder than ever. He was crying louder.

"Another slate," the holy man ordered. One of the boys ran to fetch it.

Now the holy man drew a picture of the bitten toe. He hammered the picture to a tree. Deeper and deeper he drove the spike.

But everyone could see that Mali's foot was worse than it was before.

Indira stayed outside after the others had gone back in to Mali. She was very frightened. She knew Mali was going to die. This had happened before in their village. She began to cry. She felt so helpless. It was her fault. And she had promised Mali only this morning that she would always take good care of him.

Suddenly Indira thought of the white man. She had heard that he had strange powers. He had helped sick people get well before. She knew that her parents would not like it, but Indira was desperate. Mali was going to die if she didn't do something.

She ran to the missionaries' house.

"Please come," she pleaded. "Mali has been bitten by a scorpion. He'll die if someone doesn't help him."

Grabbing up his black bag, the white man took Indira's hand and together they hurried toward her crowded hut. The villagers stepped back when they saw the white man. Many of them did not trust him.

Arjan, Indira's father, came up to them.

"What is the meaning of this? What are you doing under our roof?" he growled.

"Your daughter tells me that your son has been bitten by a scorpion. Perhaps I can help him."

Indira saw the indecision in her father's eyes. She knew how he felt about the white missionary. But she knew, too, how much he loved Mali.

"Please, Father, let him help Mali," she pleaded.

Arjan looked at Mali's red swollen foot. He looked at Indira's tear streaked face.

"Do what you can," he grunted. "It is plain to see no one else can help him." He turned away sadly, his shoulders bent.

The white man took command.

"Everyone please leave us alone," he said as he gently ushered the villagers in the direction of the door.

Indira stepped back so she would be out of the way, but she could not force herself to leave. She anxiously watched as the white man bent over Mali.

Some time later, he motioned to Indira.

"Come here, little one," he said as he beckoned to her. "See. He is resting well now. Soon he will be splashing in the pond with his friends again."

Indira placed her small dark hand in the doctor's large white one. She looked up at him shyly.

"Are you sure Mali will be all right now?" she asked.

"Yes," the doctor answered. "I think Mali will be as good as ever."

"Oh, can we ever thank you enough?" Indira asked.

"It should be easy enough," her new friend said. "Perhaps you and Mali will come to visit me. I have many things I would like to tell you."

"I think Mother and Father will let us come to see you now," Indira said. "Mali and I want to hear your stories. My friends say you speak of someone called 'Jesus.' I would like to hear about him."

Indira smiled as the doctor squeezed her hand. Then she watched him gather his belongings and leave the hut. She looked over at her sleeping brother. She sighed happily. She had kept her promise to Mali. He was going to be well soon.

And then, as soon as Mali was able, both of them would go to hear the stories of the nice white doctor. Indira knew that his Jesus must be a wonderful person if their new friend thought he was.

Bible Story: JESUS OUR SAVIOUR

God created the heavens and the earth. Then He put flowers and trees and birds and animals on the earth. After He had everything all prepared, He placed the first man on the earth. His name was Adam.

After God made Adam, He said, "Adam needs a companion." So God created a companion for Adam. Her name was Eve.

God placed Adam and Eve in a lovely garden.

He said, "Adam, you may eat everything you want in this garden except for one thing. Do not eat any of the fruit from the Tree of the Knowledge of Good and Evil. If you do, you will surely die."

And Adam disobeyed God. He ate from the Tree of the Knowledge of Good and Evil even though God had told him not to do so.

Because what God says is always true, Adam would now have to die.

Not only would Adam have to die, but all his children and their children — in fact, all the people who would ever be born — would have to die, too. Adam had brought sin into the blood of the human race.

God was very unhappy because Adam had disobeyed Him.

He didn't want Adam and the rest of the people to die. He wanted to give them another chance.

So, God made a plan. Anyone who accepted His plan would be saved.

God told Adam that He would send a Saviour to the world. This Saviour would take upon Himself all the sins of the world. Since man was not perfect, but sinful, he could not save himself. But he could accept this Saviour. Whoever accepted Him would have eternal life. Their physical bodies would still have to die, but their souls would always be with God.

God then killed some animals and made coats for Adam and Eve out of the skins. Already something had to shed its blood because of sin.

There was another tree in the Garden — the Tree of Life. If Adam would eat of the fruit of this tree, he would have to live forever in sin. God did not want to see this happen. So He sent Adam and Eve out of the Garden of Eden.

Many thousands of years later, God kept His promise to Adam. He sent the Saviour — His own Son, Jesus — who had been with Him in heaven since before the beginning of the world. He sent Him as a little baby.

He chose a young woman named Mary to be Jesus' mother.

One calm, quiet night, some shepherds were out on a hillside near Bethlehem watching their sheep.

Suddenly there was a brilliant light and an angel appeared before them.

"Don't be afraid," the angel said. "I have come to tell you some wonderful news. Today the Saviour has been born. Go to Bethlehem and see Him. You will know Him because He will be in a manger, wrapped in white cloth."

The shepherds all hurried to Bethlehem to see the Baby Jesus. They saw Mary and Mary's husband, Joseph, too.

Mary and Joseph and Jesus went to live in Egypt for two years.

Then they went to live in a little town called Nazareth.

Jesus grew up in Nazareth. He helped Joseph, and Joseph taught Him how to make cabinets and other things out of wood.

Jesus went to school in a synagogue and memorized Bible verses from the Old Testament scrolls.

When He was thirty years old, He began to preach and to tell the people how He had come to save them from their sins.

He healed sick people and made them well.

He taught everyone about God.

Many people loved Him and believed in Him, but some of the people hated Him. The ones who hated Him wanted to kill Him.

Jesus knew that they were planning on killing Him, but He didn't do anything to stop them. That was why He had left heaven and come to the earth in the first place.

Jesus could have saved Himself. He didn't have to die for us. He did it because He loves us and He knew it was the only way that we could have eternal life.

He gave His life for us. He had to shed His perfect, sinless blood for our salvation.

While Jesus was hanging on the cross, all our sins were laid on Him.

But there is something that we must do if Jesus' death is going to do us any good. We must realize that we are sinners and that we do things that displease God. We must realize that we need a Saviour. We must realize that we need to be saved from our sins, because we cannot save ourselves.

We must trust Jesus as our Saviour.

Romans 3:23 says, "The wages of sin is death, but the gift of God is eternal life through Jesus Christ our Lord."

I John 1:7 says, "The blood of Jesus Christ, God's Son, cleanseth us from all sin."

Program 11

THANKSGIVING

Scripture: Psalm 23

Object Lesson: ON BEING THANKFUL

(Object: Horn of Plenty)

This is called a Horn of Plenty. It represents how much we have for which to be thankful. See how it is overflowing? It reminds us to be grateful for all our blessings.

Each piece of fruit or vegetable can represent something for which you are thankful. I want each one of you to name to yourself something for which you are thankful each time I take out something from the Horn of Plenty.

Remember your home — parents — brothers — sisters — school — warm clothes — winter snow — friends — Sunday School — Children's Church —

Now let's go down the rows, asking each one of you to tell us something which you have thought of.

(After each child has had an opportunity to say what he wants to say, lead in a prayer of thanksgiving.)

Application Story: KENNY LEARNS TO SAY THANK YOU

This is a story about a boy who never said "Thank you."

Kenny was an only child. This meant that he had no brothers or sisters. It also meant that he didn't have to share his toys or books with anybody. Consequently, I'm afraid Kenny was just a little bit spoiled.

Any time Kenny wanted anything, he just asked for it and either his mother or his father got it for him. Kenny became so accustomed to receiving everything he wanted that he just didn't bother to say "Thank you" to anyone when he got it.

His mother and daddy told him that it was impolite not to express his gratitude, but I'm afraid that Kenny even forgot to be grateful at all most of the time.

One day Mother had a terrible pain in her side. Her doctor told her she would have to go to the hospital so he could give her a check-up and find out what was causing the pain.

Kenny had no one to be at home with him after school. So Daddy arranged to have him go home with Tommy White, one of his schoolmates who lived down the street. Then each day Daddy picked him up on his way home from work.

Kenny didn't particularly like this arrangement, but he realized that his mother wasn't sick on purpose. So he had to accept it.

One reason why Kenny didn't like to go home with Tommy was that Tommy had so many brothers and sisters. Brothers and sisters were probably fun sometimes, but they sure did keep a person from having his own way.

After school Mrs. White always set out what she wanted the children to have for a snack. It wasn't like at home where he raided the refrigerator whenever he chose.

The very first day that Kenny spent at the Whites' he noticed something unusual about the children. In fact, he noticed it every day after that, too. Sometimes Mrs. White had prepared peanut butter and jelly sandwiches. Sometimes it was an apple or an orange. But it didn't make any difference what she had for them, all of the White children kissed their mother and thanked her.

"Let's go outside and play," Tommy suggested one day.

"Okay," Kenny agreed.

Outside, they discovered a whole gang of children playing a game called "May I?" One person would say to the leader, "Johnnie, may I cross your river?" The leader would then tell that person that he could go a certain distance and how far he could go. But the player had to remember to say "May I?" before he proceeded. If he forgot, he didn't get to move ahead. The first one across the river got to be the leader for the next game.

Tommy asked the children if they could join them, and soon it was Kenny's turn.

"Johnny, may I cross your river?" he asked.

"Yes, you may take one giant step," the leader replied.

Kenny proceeded to take the giant step.

"Oh, oh, go back. You forgot to say 'May I?' All the others laughed, but Kenny didn't laugh. He didn't think it was funny!

"Let's play something else," Kenny begged.

But the other children were all having fun. They didn't pay any attention to him.

Kenny began to pout. He didn't like this game. In fact, he didn't like the Whites. He wished his mother would get well so he could go home and stay.

The next day during lunch while Kenny and Tommy were eating their sandwiches, the boys were talking.

"Kenny," Tommy said, "it has been fun having you come over to our house. I'm sorry your mother has been sick, but I'm glad to have you stay with us."

Kenny didn't bother to answer, even though he could have at least said "thank you" to Tommy.

The bell rang, and the boys went back to class.

After school, Kenny was leaning on the stone wall in front of the building waiting to meet Tommy. He heard his name mentioned. He couldn't help but listen to hear what was being said about him. He couldn't see who was talking because they were on the other side of the wall.

"Kenny Martin is staying over at your house, isn't he?" he heard a boy say.

"Yes. Until his dad picks him up after work," Kenny heard one of the White boys answer.

"Well, I'm glad he isn't coming to my house!" was the retort. "I don't think he's very nice."

"He's all right," Charlie answered. "He isn't very polite, but Mamma says he's not polite because he doesn't have brothers and sisters like we do."

"Well, maybe, but anyway, I'm glad he's at your house instead of mine!"

Kenny was embarrassed. He hadn't realized that other boys and girls thought he was impolite. In fact, he hadn't given it much thought at all.

"Hi!" called Tommy as he came out of the school. "Sorry I'm late. I stayed to help Mrs. Jackson clean the blackboards."

"That's okay," Kenny said.

The boys headed for the White home.

"Tommy," Kenny said thoughtfully. "Do you think I'm impolite?"

"Well," Tommy answered, "you aren't exactly impolite, Kenny. It's just that it seems like you don't appreciate things. You don't ever say "thank you" to anybody. Maybe you have always had so much that you aren't as thankful as we are."

"I guess I just never thought about it before," Kenny said. "I appreciate things. But I guess I don't remember to let anybody know it."

Just then the boys caught up with some of Tommy's brothers and sisters. They started talking about other things, but Kenny didn't forget what he and Tommy had been talking about. He thought it all over. He felt pretty bad about what he had learned today. He decided he was going to do something about it.

That night when Kenny's father picked him up, he noticed how quiet Kenny was.

"Anything wrong, Son?" he asked.

"No, not really, Dad. It's just that I found out something today. I've never thanked you for all you have given me and everything you have done for me. I'm sorry I haven't done it before, but I really do appreciate all the things that I get. Thank you, Dad. I'll be glad when Mom comes home so I can thank her, too."

And then Kenny added this to himself: "And from now on I'm going to thank people as soon as I have something to be thankful for. That way I won't get so far behind with my Thank You's!"

Bible Story: A SHEPHERD BOY THANKS GOD

David was a handsome sun-tanned young man who lived in the town of Bethlehem. His father's name was Jesse. David had seven brothers who were all older and bigger than he was.

Each one of the boys had a different job to do. David's job was to take care of his father's sheep. He would take his rod and staff and lead the sheep out to a good place for them to nibble the grass. Then he would sit down and watch the sheep so nothing could hurt them.

He couldn't go to sleep while he was watching the sheep. His father trusted him. He had to be alert and ready to drive away any wild animals that came.

David would sit and look up at the bright blue sky and think about how wonderful God is. He would think how God had made the whole sky and everything in it. He would think about how God had made the whole world and everything in it, too.

David talked with God while he was out in the meadow. And he sang songs. These were very special songs. They were songs that he made up himself. Some of these songs have been saved, and they are in our Bibles today, in the Book of Psalms.

Sometimes he thought of God as a Shepherd who looked after him just the way he looked after his own sheep. Then he would sing what we can read in our Bibles. It is called the Twenty-third Psalm. "The Lord is my shepherd; I shall not want. He maketh me to lie down in green pastures: he leadeth me beside the still waters. He restoreth my soul; he leadeth me in the paths of righteousness for his name's sake. Yea, though I walk through the valley of the shadow of death, I will fear no evil: for thou art with me; thy rod and thy staff they comfort me. Thou preparest a table before me in the presence of mine enemies: thou anointest my head with oil; my cup runneth over. Surely goodness and mercy shall follow me all the days of my life: and I will dwell in the house of the Lord forever."

One day, while David was singing and playing his harp, a big lion sneaked up and grabbed one of his sheep.

"Baa--aa," the little lamb cried.

David jumped up and ran over and hit the lion. He pulled the lamb out of his mouth. Then the lion charged after David, but he grabbed him by his beard and hit him and killed him. Sometimes he used his slingshot to kill the wild animals. David was very grateful to God for helping him and saving both himself and his sheep.

Another day, while David was out tending his flock, his father had a visitor whose name was Samuel.

Samuel was a prophet of God, and he had a very important job to do.

"Fill your horn with oil," God had said to Samuel. "Go to Jesse, of Bethlehem, because I have chosen one of his sons to be the next king of Israel."

Samuel obeyed God. Now he was with Jesse and with David's brothers. Samuel looked at each of the boys.

First, he looked at Eliab, David's oldest brother. No, he was not the one God had chosen.

Then he looked at Abinadab. No, he was not the one God had chosen.

Then he looked at Shammah. He was not the one God had chosen.

Samuel looked at the other four sons. None of them were God's choice.

Samuel was puzzled.

"Do you have any other sons, Jesse?" he asked. "God has not chosen any of these, but He definitely told me that He has chosen one of your sons. Do you have any more sons?"

"Why, yes," Jesse answered. "But it surely wouldn't be him. He is my youngest son, David. He's out watching the sheep. I'll send for him."

David couldn't imagine what was going on when the messenger breathlessly ran up to him.

"Hurry, David," the messenger panted. "Your father wants you."

"Please take care of my sheep until I return," David shouted over his shoulder. He ran as fast as he could to his father.

As soon as David came into sight, God told Samuel, "Anoint him, Samuel. This is the one whom I have chosen."

When David came up to the group, his father pointed to Samuel. "This man is Samuel, a prophet of God. He wants to see you."

"Kneel down before me, lad," Samuel told David.

He knelt before the old man, and he bowed his head. He knew something very important was happening.

Samuel poured the oil on David's head.

"God has chosen you to be the next king of Israel, David," Samuel told him.

After Samuel had poured the oil on David's head, the young

man stayed on his knees and kept his head bowed as he prayed to God.

"Thank you, God, for all the things you have made. Thank you for all you have done for me. And especially thank you for trusting me enough to choose me to be the next king. Amen."

We have many things to be thankful for, too. We, of course, will never be chosen to be a king because we don't have kings in our country. But God knows each one of us and He has chosen each one of us to be something very special for him. He has given us many things for which we are grateful. We must remember to thank Him for our blessings, just as David did.

Program 12

THANKSGIVING

Scripture: 2 Kings 4; 6:1-23

Object Lesson: GOD GAVE US OUR BODIES

(Object: A doll)

This doll has a body. It is nice to play with, but the doll can't do any of the things we can do. Our bodies can do all kinds of things.

Today we are going to think about all the things we can be grateful for in our bodies. God has given us our health. If we are able to be here today, we are so much better off than many boys and girls who are in hospitals or sick in bed right now.

But when we are sick, we have something to be thankful for, too. We can thank God for doctors and nurses and medicine that makes us well.

Besides our health, we can be thankful for our eyes and the ability to see all the beautiful things in the world. We can be thankful for our ears and the ability to hear sounds like birds singing and bells ringing and other people talking.

We should be thankful for the ability to taste all the good food there is to taste and to feel all the good things there are to feel.

God has given us these senses so we can enjoy things. But He has also given them to us for our protection. They warn of danger. Our eyes help us see cars in the street so we will not get run over. Our ears enable us to hear our mothers calling us to come home for dinner. Our fingers can feel when they are near something hot so we do not get burned. Our noses warn us of odors that could make us sick.

Yes, we have many things in our bodies for which we should be thankful. God has provided us with marvelous bodies. If we are really grateful for them we will take good care of them and use them for Him.

Application Story: JULIE'S THANKSGIVING

Julie gazed out of the window. She loved to watch the snow-flakes swirl in the wind and then land silently on the trees and grass. This was the first snow of the year and Julie had eagerly anticipated its arrival.

The trouble was that Julie had made plans for the first snow. She and her friends had agreed long ago that when it snowed they would all gather in the park and have a sledding party. That part was fine, except tomorrow was Thanksgiving Day and Julie had to go with her parents to her grandmother's farm for dinner. She didn't want to go; she knew all the others would be at the park, and she would miss all the fun.

"Oh, Mother, it's snowing," Julie said. "I don't want to go to Grandma's tomorrow. Why can't I stay here?"

"I know you'll have lots of fun on the farm, Julie," Mother answered. "You can take your sled with you. Danny and Rickie will probably bring theirs, too. We wouldn't want to leave you here alone. It's a family holiday, and it wouldn't be right not to have you there."

Danny and Rickie were Julie's cousins. They and all the rest of the family always went to Grandma's and Grandpa's for Thanksgiving Day.

The next morning Julie and her mother and father packed their things in the trunk of the car. Julie still wished she could stay home, but she helped all she could. She saw to it that her sled was in the trunk, too. The snow scrunched under their boots. Their cheeks were rosy from the cold. Soon everything was ready. Julie climbed into the back seat.

"Come, Pogo, Come, Pogo," she called. "We're ready to go."

The shaggy haired dog clambered into the car and Julie wiped his feet. He always got to go when they went to Grandpa's farm. He loved to run in the fields and chase the squirrels and rabbits.

The highways were cleared, but the fields glistened in the sunshine. It was a beautiful day, and Julie felt her spirits begin to lift.

When the car turned into Grandpa's driveway and headed back toward the barn, people seemed to explode from the house and surrounding buildings. Grandma and Grandpa, aunts, uncles, and cousins. Everyone was happy to see Julie and her parents.

It didn't take long to unload the trunk. The grownups went inside to finish preparing dinner and Julie and her cousins stayed out to play. The snow was just right for sledding and their snowsuits and boots kept them warm and protected.

Danny and Rickie had brought their sleds, too, and they all raced to see who was the fastest. It was fun, and Julie didn't mind that she was always last. Pogo barked excitedly as he chased the sleds.

Soon the dinner bell pealed out and summoned the children to dinner.

"Um-m-m." "How lovely!" "You brought my favorite salad." "I love the way you prepare these." The food on the table was plentiful. It looked and smelled delicious.

Grandpa said the blessing. "Dear God, we thank You for letting us all be together again this year. We thank you for our many blessings. We thank you for this dinner. Amen."

It was quiet for a while, with only the clink of silverware against china breaking the silence. Everyone was too busy eating to talk.

After a while, conversation was slowly resumed.

"Mother, these green beans are delicious," Aunt Emily praised Grandma. "And your turkey gets better every year!"

"My, how you have grown," Uncle George said to Julie. "It seems like you've grown five inches since we last saw you!"

"Well, not quite, Uncle George, but almost," Julie answered.

After the pumpkin pie piled high with whipped cream was served and eaten, everyone carried his own dishes to the kitchen. Julie helped the ladies clean up and soon they were all in the front room seated around the fire which was crackling and spitting sparks.

"Thanksgiving Day is a good day," Grandpa said. "It is good that it is set aside as a holiday by our government. There's no better time for us all to get together and praise God for all our blessings."

"Let's all tell of some of the things we are thankful for," Grandma suggested. "You be first, George, and we'll go around the room."

"Well," Uncle George smiled as he talked. "We all have many things to be thankful for, I'm sure. But I guess one of the things I'm most thankful for this year is my new job."

"I'm thankful for my new washing machine and dryer," Aunt Ellen said. "They are so nice. They save me so much work."

"I'm thankful for the good health we've all had this past year," Julie's mother contributed.

Each took his turn and finally they were all waiting for Julie to speak.

She hardly knew how to start. Clearing her throat, she began, "Well, I think I'm thankful most of all for my family. I'm thankful we can sit down here together after Thanksgiving dinner and just be here together, like this. I'm grateful for a family that has helped me to learn to be thankful. We are so much happier when we appreciate what we have. I'm glad I came."

And then it was Grandpa's turn, and he was last.

"I think that just about covers everything," he said. "We do have much to thank God for."

Everyone nodded in agreement, and then they bowed their heads in prayer. They silently thanked God for all their blessings and praised Him for them.

After a brief pause, Danny broke the silence.

"Let's go out and ride our sleds," he urged.

Julie jumped up to get her wraps. It was fun to play in the snow with her cousins. And besides, it had snowed so much that there would be plenty left in the park for the rest of the weekend. She really was glad she had come.

Bible Story: ELISHA'S MIRACLES

Elisha was a great prophet. Elisha talked to God. God talked with Elisha.

God allowed him to do things no one else could do. Because he did these things, the people believed Elisha and listened to him. He told the people what God wanted them to know.

One time Elisha helped a woman whose husband was dead. She was very poor. She had many bills she could not pay.

"Help me, Elisha," the widow begged. "You know my husband was a good man who feared God. Now I owe so much money that the people that I owe the money to are going to take away my two sons and make them slaves."

"What can I do for you?" Elisha asked. "Tell me, what do you have in your house?"

"All I have is one pot of oil," the widow answered.

"Go to your neighbors and borrow all the empty pots and pans and barrels and buckets you can find," Elisha told her.

Trip after trip the widow and her sons made to all her neighbors' houses. After a while, she came back to Elisha.

"We have every single empty pot and pan that our neighbors own. What shall we do now, Elisha?"

"You and your sons go into that room where all the empty pans are. Pour oil from your vessel into them. When one pan is full, set it aside and fill the next one. Then when that pan is full, set it aside and fill the next — and the next — and the next."

The woman and her sons went into the room and closed the door. She started pouring the oil. She poured and poured. She filled one pan, then she filled another. She filled a pan and then called for another. And all this oil came out of the single pot of oil she had owned in the first place!

After a while, she said, "Go get me the rest of the empty pans."

"But, Mother, they are all filled!" her sons told her.

Sure enough, every pan was full to the brim.

They went outside and called Elisha.

"Look, Elisha, all the pots and barrels and pans are full of oil," the woman told the prophet.

"Good," he answered. "Now go and sell the oil. Use the money to pay your bills. Now you and your sons will not be bothered because you can pay all your bills with the money you get when you sell the oil."

Another time, Elisha brought a boy back to life. When the boy had died, his mother had run for Elisha.

"Come, Elisha," the mother begged. "My son has died."

Elisha went to the home of the boy. He went into the house and saw the boy lying on the bed.

Elisha went back to the door and closed it. He prayed to God. He went over and lay upon the boy. He put his mouth on the boy's mouth. He put his eyes upon the boy's eyes. He put his hands upon the boy's hands. He stretched his whole body upon the boy's body.

The boy's body became warm. But he didn't move.

Elisha got up. He paced back and forth.

Then he went back to the boy's body and stretched himself upon it once again.

This time the boy sneezed seven times and opened his eyes. He was alive again!

Elisha performed many miracles. And he always let the people know that it was really God who did these things; He was just using Elisha. Elisha didn't take credit for any of the miracles, because he knew that he could not have done them without God.

Another time, he caused an iron ax head to float.

One of his friends had borrowed an ax and was chopping wood with it when the head of the ax flew off and landed in the water.

"Oh, no," the friend cried, "the ax was borrowed. It wasn't even mine!"

"Where did it fall?" Elisha asked him.

"Right over there."

The man pointed to the river. He threw a stick over the place to show where it had fallen into the water.

Just then, the ax head bobbed up to the top.

"There's your ax head," Elisha said.

Another time that Elisha had something unusual happen was when he and his servant seemed to be in a lot of trouble.

Syria was at war with Israel.

A strange thing was happening. Every time the king of Syria talked about his war plans to his officers, the king of Israel knew everything he had said.

The Syrians couldn't sneak up on the Israelites, because the Israelites always knew what the Syrians' plans were.

"We have a spy among us," the king of Syria shouted. "Who is he?"

"No, we don't have a spy, your highness. It's Elisha, a prophet in Israel. He tells the king of Israel everything you say."

"Go get him and bring him to me," the king ordered.

The king sent many men with many horses and chariots to Dothan to get Elisha.

When it was dark, they surrounded the city.

Elisha and his servant got up the next morning. The servant went outside. He saw all the soldiers around the city. He was frightened. He ran in to Elisha.

"The Syrian soldiers have come to get us! What shall we do?"

"Do not be afraid," Elisha answered. "There are more on our side than on theirs."

"What do you mean?" the young servant asked.

Elisha prayed. "Lord, I pray thee, open his eyes so he can see how you are protecting us."

God opened the eyes of the servant so he could see something that he had not been able to see before.

Oh! It was a marvelous sight! The mountain was full of horses and chariots of fire.

The young man knew that God was protecting them.

Then Elisha prayed again.

"Lord, make these Syrians blind."

God made all the Syrian soldiers blind.

Elisha went out to them.

"This isn't the way," he told them. "I'll take you to the man you are looking for."

Then he led them to Samaria, the capital city of Israel, in which the king lived.

He prayed again. "Now, Lord, let them see again."

The Lord opened their eyes. They looked all around them.

"We've been tricked!" they cried.

Now they were the ones who were afraid!

"What shall I do with them?" the king of Israel asked Elisha.

"Don't hurt them," Elisha told him. "Feed them and let them return home."

"And the king prepared great provision for them. And when they had eaten and drunk, he sent them away, and they went to their master. So the bands of Syria came no more into the land of Israel" (2 Kings 6:23).

Program 13

CHRISTMAS

Scripture: Luke 2:8-20

Object Lesson: CHRISTMAS CAROLS

(Object: Song book)

Singing songs is one of the ways we praise God. It is one of the ways we celebrate Christmas. We sing special songs at Christmastime. We call them Christmas carols.

Christmas carols tell us about the birth of Jesus. They tell of his sleeping in a manger. They tell about the little town of Bethlehem where He was born. They tell us about the wise men and the shepherds and the angels.

We sing because our hearts are glad. We sing because we want God to know how much we appreciate His sending His Son, Jesus, to be born as a baby.

When we sing, we worship God. I am glad He gave us voices so we can sing. Aren't you?

Application Story: BECKY'S LOVE GIFT

Becky Riley was ten years old. It was almost Christmas, and Becky was very happy. For, you see, this Christmas Becky had something very special to be happy about. She had let Jesus come into her heart during the past year.

She had learned about Jesus and all that He had done for her. She learned how He had been born in a little town called Bethlehem and how the angels had sung at His birth. She learned that Jesus was born of the virgin Mary and that God was His Father.

Jesus was different from any other man who had ever lived on earth — He was both man and God.

117

Jesus told everyone that He had come to save them from their sins so they could have eternal life with God. He told them that He was going to be killed but that He would not stay dead. He said that He would overcome death and be the Saviour of everyone who believed in Him.

Becky was glad she had let Jesus come into her heart. Since then everything had been different for her. She didn't look any different on the outside, but she felt different on the inside. Every day she asked God to help her to be a good Christian. Every once in a while she did something that was bad, but she always told God she was sorry and asked Him to forgive her.

Becky lived with her mother who was away at work most of the time. She prayed every night that God would help her mother to love Jesus, too.

Every Saturday night when she took her bath and laid out her clean clothes for Sunday School she invited her mother to go with her. But it never seemed as if she could.

On the Sunday before Christmas Becky got ready as usual.

"Mother, will you please go to church with me today?" she asked. "It's Christmas Sunday and there will be pretty music. You'll like it."

"Not today, Becky," Mother said, "but I will go with you Christmas Eve to the Children's Worship Service if you'd like."

"Oh! Would I!" Becky exclaimed. "I'll tell my teacher, Mrs. Patterson, you're coming! I know she'll be glad, too!"

At Sunday School everyone talked about the Christmas love offering. On Christmas Eve an offering was going to be taken for the missionaries. The boys and girls were asked to bring what money they could. They could also bring good, clean clothing they had outgrown, canned food, and toys that were not broken or could be easily repaired.

Becky dreaded the offering. She didn't have any money. It took every penny her mother made to pay the apartment rent and buy their food. As far as clothes were concerned, they were almost worn out by the time Becky herself got them.

As Christmas Eve approached, Becky was first happy, then sad. She was happy because it was Jesus' birthday. And she was happy, too, because her mother was going to the Christmas Eve program with her. It was going to be so nice to have her mother there to hear her as she recited the Christmas story from Luke.

But Becky was sad because she was concerned about her love gift to Jesus. She didn't know what she could give. And she did so very much want to give something very, very nice and special to show Jesus how much she loved Him.

Monday came and went. Becky still didn't know what to do about the offering.

Tuesday came and went. She still didn't know what to do about the offering.

Wednesday came. The Christmas Eve Worship Service would be tonight.

School was out at noon on Christmas Eve day. Becky came home and fixed herself a sandwich for lunch. Then she began to think about what she needed to do to get ready for Christmas. She was giving only one present — an apron which she had made secretly and kept hidden from her mother. It was neatly wrapped and tied with one of her hair ribbons. She had her Bible verses memorized for the church program.

But she still did not have her missionary love offering.

Becky went into the bedroom she shared with her mother. She lay across the clean spread and tried to think. She hugged her doll, Peggy, close to her.

"Peggy," she said, "I sure do wish I could figure out something to give to the missionary love offering tonight. Jesus has done so much for me and I love Him so much. What shall I do?"

Peggy's pretty doll face smiled back at Becky. Becky hugged her close. She didn't have many toys, but Peggy made up for them all. She liked to make clothes for her and dress her. And she even liked to talk to her because she was alone so much of the time.

Still holding Peggy tightly, Becky slipped off the bed onto her knees. She bowed her head and closed her eyes.

"Dear God," she prayed, "please show me what I can give to Jesus for His birthday. I cannot think of anything that is good enough except Peggy, and I could not possibly give her away."

Just then Becky thought of a Bible verse she had learned in Sunday School. "With God all things are possible."

"But Peggy's all I've got," she said.

Then she thought of another verse.

"God so loved the world that he gave his only begotten Son that whosoever believeth in him should not perish but have everlasting life."

" 'God so loved the world that he gave his only begotten Son,' " she repeated slowly.

God gave His only Son for me, Becky thought. Aloud she said, "I love you so much, Peggy."

She hugged the smiling doll close to her.

"Mamma!" Peggy cried.

Becky's heart began to pound. Suddenly she felt better. She knew what she was going to do.

Peggy would go in the missionary basket.

"You'll make some little missionary girl very happy, and she will make you happy, too," Becky promised Peggy. "I must hurry and wash your clothes so they'll be nice and clean. You'll want to look your very best!"

All afternoon Becky washed and ironed Peggy's clothes. She mended all the tears in the seams. She scrubbed the doll's face until it was rosy and shining. Then, as time for the program drew near, Becky packed the clothes in a large brown paper sack. Last of all, she put Peggy in. Here was a present that Jesus would like, Becky thought. A present which would show Him how much she really loved Him.

Mrs. Riley was late getting home from work. Becky was ready to go to the program. Mrs. Riley didn't take time to eat, but she washed her face and combed her hair.

"I'm ready, Becky. Let's go to church," she said.

Hurriedly they departed.

The program was gay and festive, ending in a silent worship period. Then, one by one, those who had love gifts went forward to place their gifts before the manger scene in the front of the room.

Becky smiled at her mother. "I'll be right back," she whispered. Then she went forward. She laid her paper bag down and started to leave. After a pause, however, she stepped back and reached into the sack and pulled out Peggy. She kissed the doll and gently lay her on top of the sack.

Becky smiled broadly. She was happy to give Jesus her best. After all, had He not given His best for her?

Becky didn't notice the tears in her mother's eyes.

At the close of the program, the preacher quietly spoke. "We have seen a real presentation of love tonight. I am wondering if there is anyone here who has not already done so who would like to give himself to Jesus. We'll wait for you to come while the pianist plays one verse of 'Silent Night.'"

Quiet fell upon the congregation. Everyone bowed his head and closed his eyes. Becky felt a movement beside her. She opened her eyes and turned to her mother. Mrs. Riley had risen from her chair.

"I'm going to go up and give my life to Jesus," she said to Becky. "Would you like to go with me?"

Becky smiled and took her mother's hand. The woman and the little girl moved to the front.

Becky thought she had been happy before, when she had given her love gift to Jesus. Now her happiness seemed to bubble over and spill out.

This was the happiest Christmas a girl could possibly have had!

EPILOGUE

That night, long after Becky had gone to bed, Mrs. Riley heard a soft knock on the front door. Answering it, she was met by Mr. Patterson, the husband of Becky's Sunday School teacher. He handed Mrs. Riley a box.

"It's for Becky," he said. "We hope she likes it. We hope you have a happy Christmas!"

He turned and started down the apartment steps.

"Thank you so much," Mrs. Riley called after him. "I know we will."

Carefully she carried the box over to the little Christmas tree in front of the window. As she lay the package down, Mrs. Riley smiled. From inside the box she had heard a faint "mamma."

Yes, indeed, this was going to be a happy Christmas!

Bible Story: THE FIRST CHRISTMAS CAROLS

It was night. It was dark. It was over 1900 years ago.

The shepherds were out in the pasture. That day they had taken their sheep to where they could get plenty of green grass to eat. It was too far to go back home for the night, so they just lay down on the grass to rest and sleep.

The sheep were settling down.

The men had built a fire, and they were quietly talking to each other. They talked about many things. They talked about their families. They talked about their sons and what the boys were learning at the synagogue. They talked about God, too.

They looked up at the clear sky above them. They saw the moon and thousands and thousands of tiny stars up there.

"Just think," one of the shepherds said, "how wonderful God is. He made us and everything on the earth, too. He even made the moon and all those stars up there."

They all looked at the stars and at the moon.

"Yes, God is wonderful," they agreed.

Suddenly, there was a bright light all around them!

They jumped to their feet.

At first they couldn't see, the light was so bright. They rubbed their eyes. Then, they could see an angel standing before them!

The shepherds were frightened. They didn't know what was happening. None of them had ever seen an angel before! They didn't know whether to run or to stay where they were!

"Do not be afraid," the angel said. "Nothing is going to hurt you. I have come to tell you some good news. Today a little baby was born in Bethlehem. This baby is the Son of God.

"Go to Bethlehem and see Him. You will know Him because He will be wrapped in swaddling clothes and He will be lying in a manger in a stable."

Then the angel was no longer alone. There were many angels around him. They all started to sing.

"Glory to God in the highest," they sang. "And on earth, peace, goodwill toward men."

The shepherds had never heard such a beautiful song or such beautiful music. They all just stood there, looking and listening.

When the angels finished their song, they went back to heaven.

The bright light faded. It was dark again. The stars twinkled in the sky. It was very quiet.

The shepherds didn't speak for a minute. They just stood there, thinking of the bright light and the beautiful angels and the wonderful news that they had heard.

Finally, one of them broke the silence.

"Let's go to Bethlehem! Let's go see this thing that the Lord has made known to us."

Quickly they all called their sheep, and they started toward Bethlehem.

They couldn't travel fast enough, they were so excited! Soon they came to the little town.

Then they looked for a stable, because the angel had told them that the baby would be in a manger in a stable. It didn't take them long to find the right one. They knew it was the right one, because there was the baby, lying in a manger. And the baby was wrapped in a long clean cloth, just as the angel had said.

Close by the baby's side was a man and a woman. The woman was Mary, the mother of the baby. The man was Joseph, Mary's husband.

Reverently, the shepherds walked up to the manger. They looked at the sweet little baby.

One of them explained to Mary and Joseph why they had come. "We knew the Christ Child was here because angels from God came to us out in the field and told us. There was a bright light and the angels sang a beautiful song. They told us how we could recognize the Christ Child. They said He would be wrapped in swaddling clothes and lying in a manger."

The shepherds knelt down beside the Baby Jesus. They bowed their heads and prayed.

"Thank You, God, for sending Your angels to us to tell us about the Baby Jesus," they prayed. "Thank You for Your great love for us. Thank You for sending Your Son to be our Saviour."

They got up from their knees and turned to Mary and Joseph.

"Thank you for letting us worship the Christ Child," they said. "We shall never forget what we have heard and seen this night."

The shepherds went out of the stable, rejoicing and singing praises to God. They told everybody that came along their way about the angels and about what the angels had told them. They told them about the Baby Jesus.

First, the angels had sung a song about the birth of the Baby Jesus.

Then, the shepherds sang a song about the birth of the Baby Jesus.

And now we sing songs about the birth of the Baby Jesus.

They are very special songs that we sing at Christmas time. We call them "Christmas carols."

Closing Prayer

As we leave our Children's Church,
   Help us, Lord, we pray,
To remember things we've learned
   And use them every day.
      In Jesus' Name, Amen.